MW00625186

Del has put together a fabul[...] life. I loved his stories of old professionals. I love his "Tee [...] words of wisdom that can be [...] golfer and non-golfer alike. So many wonderful truths for golf and life are woven into his writings, which base their foundation on a dynamic interactive friendship with Jesus. He's got all the bases covered from the First Tee to the Last Putt. You're going to love it!

> —Wally Armstrong, PGA Tour lifetime member, inventor, golf coach, coauthor of best-selling books *In His Grip* and *The Mulligan*

I love to play golf, watch golf, listen to commentary on golf, and read about golf. Now, I can infuse my Christian faith with this beautifully written devotional by Del Duduit featuring a deep dive into the hearts of my favorite golf professionals. Get *Birdies, Bogeys, and Blessings* and you'll SEE a Light shine brighter in your heart on the course and in the game of life. Enjoy!

> —Jim Schneider, cofounder of Eyes of Faith Optical and ZIVAH Sunglasses

Del Duduit's devotional work, *Birdies, Bogeys, and Blessings*, poignantly presents life lessons through the correlation of golf and Christianity. His personal discourse with links legends Jack Nicklaus, Stewart Cink, and Matt Kuchar, among others, passionately drives this book from tee to green. This is an inspiring read for those duffers who love the game and rejoice in the Word as much as I do.

> —Jay Miller, teacher, Scioto Tech; sportscaster, WTZP

More Books by Del Duduit

Stars of the Faith Series
Dugout Devotions
Dugout Devotions II
First Down Devotions
First Down Devotions II
Sports Shorts

Alabama Devotions
Auburn Devotions
Florida Devotions
Florida State Devotions

BIRDIES, BOGEYS, AND BLESSINGS

30 Days of Devotions for the Godly Golfer

DEL DUDUIT

Birmingham, Alabama

BIRDIES, BOGEYS, AND BLESSINGS

Iron Stream
An imprint of Iron Stream Media
100 Missionary Ridge
Birmingham, AL 35242
IronStreamMedia.com

Library of Congress Control Number: 2023930932

Cover design by twoline || Studio

ISBN: 978-1-56309-637-2 (paperback)
ISBN: 978-1-56309-638-9 (e-book)

1 2 3 4 5—28 27 26 25 24

This book is dedicated to AJ for the positive impact you've had in my life.

Contents

Foreword

While many athletes are remembered for the records they set, most are immortalized by the number of titles they've won—Michael Jordan, Tom Brady, Jack Nicklaus, Tiger Woods.

In the sports writing world, we've read the words of some of the greats who have written about those accomplishments—Paul Zimmerman, Peter King, Frank Deford, Rick Reilly, to name a few.

And Del Duduit.

An award-winning writer who has covered the Cincinnati Bengals through the team's highs and lows and penned the best-sellers *Dugout Devotions* and *First-Down Devotions*, Duduit has given us another winner.

Duduit takes us inside the ropes into the lives of the Christian golfers on the PGA Tour. *Birdies, Bogeys, and Blessings* is full of drives down the middle of the fairways, greens in regulation, and one putts. Duduit expertly ties together each golfer's faith and how they have leaned on it to get through a difficult time on the golf course or in life.

I first met Del at a writers conference in 2016. Being a former journalist who had transitioned to book publishing, Del picked my brain during a number of the meals, after workshops, and in the hallway walking from one workshop to the next or on the way to a meal. To say he was relentless would be an understatement.

After the conference, he went his way and I went mine—both back into our writing and editing worlds. Then he released his first book in 2017, and another in 2018, and two more in 2019. I noticed, and so did others. With good reasons.

Because of his journalism background, Del knows how to make others feel at ease, pull information out of them, and string their words together in sentences and paragraphs that make the reader feel like they have cozied up next to the athlete and are enjoying their favorite beverages together.

So, it's no surprise that Del has penned another winner. He is a winner, just like the immortals—Jordan, Brady, Nicklaus, and Woods.

—Larry J. Leech II
Writing Coach and Editor of award-winning authors

Acknowledgments

Several people played a role in making this book a reality. I would like to thank the following for their efforts in bringing *Birdies, Bogeys, and Blessings* to you.

My wife, Angie, for her love, support, and suggestions.

My agent, Cyle Young, for his partnership in my career.

My publisher, John Herring, for his belief in me.

My editors Larry Leech and Susan Cornell for making this book better.

My friend and sports editor Jacob Smith for his help and connections.

My promotion team at ISM and Kim McCulla for her efforts.

My Lord and Savior Jesus Christ for this exciting opportunity.

Chapter 1

WHAT SIN IS YOUR BAG?

Stewart Cink

For by grace you have been saved through faith. And this is not your own doing; it is the gift of God, not a result of works, so that no one may boast.

—Ephesians 2:8–9

At the Memorial Tournament in 2022, a young fan sought out Stewart Cink between the practice tee and practice putting green. "Stu, Stu, sign this please," the fan said.

Cink, the 2009 Open Champion, inked a couple of flags and some golf balls and a hat.

"Thanks, Stu! Thanks, Stu, good luck this weekend," said the giddy fan.

"What's that feel like?" I said while we walked and talked toward the putting green. "How do you feel when kids want your autograph?"

"When that kind of stuff stops happening, that's when my job is in trouble."

In 2008, Stewart climbed to sixth in the Official World Golf Rankings after he won the Travelers Championship in June. The next year, he defeated Tom Watson by six strokes in a four-hole playoff at the 138th Open Championship for his first Major on the PGA Tour.

That win at Turnberry, Scotland, was brilliant. Watson, who had won The Open five times, bogeyed the seventy-second hole, while Cink birdied to force the playoff. He walked to the first tee of what would be a four-hole playoff with faith in his swing and in his heavenly Father.

Cink knows he is not a perfect golfer nor a perfect person. He is flawed just like you and me.

"At some point," he said on our short stroll together at Muirfield Village Golf Club, "you just experience things in your life that you just can't do yourself. There are things in life you just cannot overcome. When that happens, you, as a human, tend to be overwhelmed yourself."

That is when you might realize any shortcoming you may have.

"That's when you realize those flaws to a point where you start looking for something to make up for those short-comings," he added. "For me, Jesus Christ is the answer for any question or shortcoming I have. He's the answer for everything. I cannot do this by myself . . . I just can't."

His biggest shortcoming?

"That's simple—sin," Stewart said. "I have many short-comings I cannot get past. It's just sin. But I'm thankful that Jesus forgave me, and forgives me, of my sin. I'm not a Christian because I want to do things or want to win tournaments. I'm a Christian because I asked Jesus Christ to forgive me of my sins and redeem me."

Cink didn't win for another eleven years until he captured the Safeway Open. Then in 2021, he won the RBC Heritage Classic for the third time.

He never lost faith in his ability as a player or in his Lord and Savior.

"My faith is everything to me . . . and to my wife," he said. "It's a journey we are on together."

What are your shortcomings?

Casting all your anxieties on him, because he cares for you.
—1 Peter 5:7

Tee It Up

I am confident you have some good qualities, but let's focus on the shortcomings. Don't be too hard on yourself but take a few moments to look at areas of growth you may have. Maybe on this list you will find words such as *selfish, lazy, shy, strict, greedy, stubborn, impulsive, passive, lethargic, blunt, bossy, unorganized, fearful, aggressive, cheater, argumentative, workaholic,* and so on. Do any of these adjectives sound familiar? Are there more?

Sometimes a golfer can get into a funk and not hit the ball as well as they would like. Most of the time it's because of something small, something fixable through the help of their coach or range work.

Go for the Green

Everyone has flaws—areas of opportunity to improve. But Stewart said it best when he said, "I cannot do this by myself." Maybe you are facing some tough choices. Perhaps you are aware of some of your imperfections and can't make improvements. Maybe recent events in life have you feeling like you quadruple-putted the easiest hole, and you don't know what to do or where to go.

Some suggestions on how to make the best improvement you'll ever make in life:

1. Identify your weakness. You can't fix it if you don't know what it is. This takes honesty and a deep look into your characteristics. This is the first step. That is when you can make the needed changes. God won't help you if you don't admit the problem. He won't just take it away. You must lay it on the altar and give it to Him.

2. Overcome your weakness. Get into the Word of God and see what Scripture can reveal to you. Within the pages, you will find a balm that will help you heal. You will find comfort and direction. The Lord's heart will be revealed, as well as your own. All the good and bad that is within you comes from your heart. When the negative is brought to light, the wound is open to be healed.

   How can a young man keep his way pure?
       By guarding it according to your word.
   With my whole heart I seek you;
       let me not wander from your commandments!
   I have stored up your word in my heart,
       that I might not sin against you. (Psalm 119:9–11)

3. Become stronger through prayer. A golfer won't improve if he or she doesn't talk to a coach and

take instructions. The same goes for you. If you do not seek God in prayer and communicate with Him, then He will not give you much-needed direction. This can only come through spending time with Jesus in prayer. Remember, the Lord is not a wishing well. Thank Him for His blessings and listen, listen, listen to His sweet, small voice. "Be strong, and let your heart take courage, all you who wait for the LORD!" (Psalm 31:24).

4. Be determined to succeed. No one wants to fail. The loss of a job. The loss of a relationship. The loss of friends. All those can provide determination to succeed.

5. Maintain fellowship with like-minded believers. Be part of a group that will hold one another accountable. This will help all involved to become better Christians. "Whoever walks with the wise becomes wise, but the companion of fools will suffer harm" (Proverbs 13:20).

Stewart was open about his faith because it's important to him and his wife. He knows his weakness and describes it as sin. He was not specific, but he didn't have to be. The Bible says in Romans 3:23, "for all have sinned and fall short of the glory of God."

Find your weakness and humbly give it to God so He can strengthen you for the next round.

Chapter 2

ALWAYS BE HONEST WITH GOD AND YOURSELF

Cameron Tringale

The integrity of the upright shall guide them: but the perverseness of transgressors shall destroy them.
—Proverbs 11:3 (KJV)

Who would have known? Who would have cared?

Cameron Tringale was not in contention to win the 2014 PGA Championship.

The Georgia Tech product tapped in a gimme three-inch putt on the par-3 eleventh hole for a bogey on the final round on Sunday at the Valhalla Golf Course at Cumberland Center, Maine. Cameron posted a two-under-par round of 69 to finish at four under par.

Rory McIlroy left everyone in the dust and took home the major tournament with a score of sixteen under par for his fourth Major and ninth overall win at the time.

Six days later, Cameron contacted the PGA of America and admitted that he signed an incorrect scorecard and asked to be disqualified. He felt his putter, on his putt on the eleventh hole, swung over the ball before he actually hit the ball. According to PGA rules, that consists of a stroke.

This bothered him, and he thought about it for days.

The tournament was long over, and no one, not even his playing partner that day, questioned the putt.

A month later, he said to a reporter at ESPN, "While approaching the hole to tap in my three-inch bogey putt, the putter swung over the ball prior to tapping in. Realizing that there could be the slightest doubt that the swing over the ball should have been recorded as a stroke, I spoke with the PGA of America and shared with them my conclusion that the stroke should have been recorded. I regret any inconvenience this has caused the PGA of America and my fellow competitors in what was a wonderful championship."

Integrity and honesty matter. In golf and in life.

"Simply put," Tringale told me after a practice round at the 2022 Memorial Tournament, "we are all called to work hard, do everything we do for the glory of God, and I try to do that. I work hard, and I try to set a good example. When I get the chance to share about Jesus, I do that. A lot of people care about golf and about what I have to say and so I use my platform to glorify the Lord. The bottom line is that we give the Lord the glory no matter what happens."

Let's pretend for argument's sake that someone did witness Cameron's phantom putt. What would they have thought about his integrity and honesty? Did he cheat? I wonder what those people would have thought after he clarified what really happened.

Golf is a funny game. It's the only sport where you call goofs or violations on yourself.

Tringale was frustrated with the round and just wanted to get it over with. But someone saw what he did.

God.

And He whispered in Cameron's ear to make it right.

In the end, the Lord received glory and Cameron gained more respect from fans and colleagues. He set the best example of what a Christian should be.

If any man among you seem to be religious, and bridleth not his tongue, but deceiveth his own heart, this man's religion is vain.
—James 1:26 (KJV)

Tee It Up

What would you have done? Would you have called a penalty on yourself days after it was over? Would you have felt that you got away with it? You may not ever play for a major championship on the PGA Tour, but you run into similar situations every day. Do you put in an honest day's work, or do you cut out at times and leave early? Would you tell your boss and run the risk of getting docked pay? Or if the cashier made a mistake and handed you an extra $5 in change, would you give it back? Or when you play golf with your buddies, do you put down your *actual* score or not count strokes for a lost ball, ball out of bounds, or a ball in the water?

Go for the Green

J. C. Watts Jr. once said, "Character is doing the right thing when nobody's looking. Too many people think the only thing that's right is to get by, and the only thing that's wrong is to get caught." Doing the right thing may have some consequences. For Cameron, he was disqualified from a tournament for a mistake he admitted to the governing body of the event. That's honesty. Having a conversation about the truth can be a challenge, especially if you're talking with yourself. In case you need to have a heart-to-heart with a friend, here are some suggestions on how to approach the truth in love.

1. Have the conversation. Although this is a tough first move, it must happen. Never ambush someone or catch them off guard. Seek the Lord's grace and wisdom. When you know you must have this conversation, it is scary because you don't know what the outcome will be. Empathy, kindness, and love are essential when you talk to a friend about a touchy issue. "Finally, be ye all of one mind, having compassion one of another, love as brethren, be pitiful, be courteous" (1 Peter 3:8 KJV).

2. Initiate the chat and be positive. Make sure you tell the person what you admire or like about them. Try not to use words like *disappointment* or *embarrassment*. Those words can cause damage. This is not a time to joke around, but it's also not a time to kick someone when they might be down. Pray for the right words. "Wherefore comfort yourselves together, and edify one another, even as also ye do" (1 Thessalonians 5:11 KJV).

3. Make the person aware that this might be difficult to hear. There are times when facts might be

difficult to reveal. Make sure you can back up allegations with facts. Let them know the situation and what you know firsthand and give the person the benefit of the doubt.

4. Get to the point and learn. Don't beat around the bush and try to sugarcoat the topic. Putting off the conversation makes it harder as time goes by. Getting past the difficult or uncomfortable situation gets easier after you ask for forgiveness and receive it.

5. Never hold a grudge and forgive. A fresh start is always in order. Everyone makes mistakes and everyone longs for forgiveness. "And be ye kind one to another, tenderhearted, forgiving one another, even as God for Christ's sake hath forgiven you" (Ephesians 4:32 KJV).

Cameron's decision to call a penalty on himself and ask to be disqualified was all God. No one would have known, and unless a fan recorded the shot, there is no way to determine if he actually swung the putter over the ball. But it bothered him to the point where he had to make it right. No matter who knew. That's character.

He did the right thing, and the Lord was glorified.

Chapter 3

INSTILL LOVE, RESPECT, AND A GOOD WORK ETHIC

Jason Day

Everyone must submit to governing authorities. For all authority comes from God, and those in positions of authority have been placed there by God.

—Romans 13:1 (NLT)

Respect is earned through a solid work ethic. Nothing is handed to you in life.

Jason Day knows all about this philosophy. After all he's been through, he is a fighter. Throughout his life he's overcome many adversities—from losing his dad at the age of twelve and being a poor, reckless teenager to going through several illnesses and injuries. But he never let that deter him. Setbacks motivated him to have a stubborn work ethic.

His preround warm-up routine is amazing. It consists of forty-two full swings, twenty-six chip shots, and twenty-seven putts.

The Australian-born golfer has played golf most of his life and earned the respect of his colleagues.

He is a past number-one-ranked golfer in the world.

In 2011, he broke into the top ten in the World Golf Rankings after he finished runner-up in the US Open.

Three years later he brought home his first WGC-Accenture Match Play Championship. He won it again in 2016. The previous year, he won the 2015 PGA Championship—a coveted major win.

His good nature, combined with his trademark "G'day, Mate," has made him a favorite among peers and his fans.

He and his wife, Ellie, have four children, and they have a solid concept of what it takes to be a winner inside the family clubhouse.

"I just think it helps to have two parents who make sure there is a lot of love in the house to go around to everyone," he said, referring to that because he wasn't able to have that blessing past the age of twelve. "Our kids need that. And there also needs to be an authority figure with boundaries and rules. That's the best way to set the kids up for success. That way you instill in them love, respect, and hard work. My job is to pass that along and show them the right way."

Pray this way for kings and all who are in authority so that we can live peaceful and quiet lives marked by godliness and dignity.

—1 Timothy 2:2 (NLT)

Tee It Up

You may have kids who have already grown and left the house. Or you might be a young parent with a child on the way. Or you might still be too young to have a family but plan to in the future. In any situation, it's never too late to show love, respect, and a good work ethic.

Go for the Green

Life moves fast and furious, especially if you have little ones to raise. Jobs seem to take more than forty hours per week, and there are many distractions along the way. The devil wants nothing more than for you to neglect your children. If you wander and get lost in the hustle and bustle, then he will slither in and try to grab their attention. You must make plans for your children and let them know how important they are to you.

Some suggestions to help you make them a priority:

1. Time with God. When you disconnect from the world for a few minutes a day and make the Lord a priority, little eyes see this. When you take time to read your Bible and pray every day, that sets a wonderful example for kids of any age. It's never a bad idea to put Christ first in front of your children. God deserves your time, money, and everything else. Ask yourself: Does the devil want you to spend time with the Savior?

2. Family prayer and devotions. Take time to gather as a family at least once a week outside of church. You could also do this on an individual basis if it's more convenient and conducive to schedules. Read devotionals and pray with your children. If they are older, ask them to pray. Make sure they understand

that they can pray anywhere because God is every-where. This will strengthen their personal relation-ship with the Lord and encourage them to see the power of prayer. "Train up a child in the way he should go: and when he is old, he will not depart from it" (Proverbs 22:6 KJV).

3. Discuss the good and the bad. Every kid loves to hear about their strengths, but not too many want to be told their weaknesses. You are unique, and so are your children. Make sure they know that and accept who they are in the eyes of the Lord. Encourage them in their strengths and help them in their areas of growth. When you do this, you become a source of respect and admiration. Let them see the love of Jesus in you. Show them that the Lord loves them in their victories and defeats and shows grace through it all. "So encourage each other and build each other up, just as you are already doing" (1 Thessalonians 5:11 NLT).

4. Speak truth and establish boundaries. Discipline is a tough act, but it must be done. When a child is disobedient, a parent must discipline without breaking the child's spirt. When you must correct, make sure the child understands the why and the need for immediate action. I remember being told to wait until my father got home. That was tor-ture and created fear—but in the end it worked. Fear is a great motivator. But tell them the truth and enforce your rules. A leader is not a tyrant. A leader will inspire and motivate through example.

"Better to be patient than powerful; better to have self-control than to conquer a city" (Proverbs 16:32 NLT).

5. Be there. I remember my parents were always at my ball games and cheered me on. They had faults of their own, but I knew that if I looked up in the stands, I'd find them. Be in the moment, and if work calls, take the call after the game. Work can wait.

Jason makes time for his family. He has a job that calls for him to work long hours on weekends when he plays. But he also knows that his wife has his back. They raise their kids together. Take your children to church. Let them see you praise the Lord and spend time in His Word. You can't raise children on your own.

It takes a family—the family of God.

Chapter 4

A REASON TO SMILE

Matt Kuchar

A merry heart maketh a cheerful countenance.
                              —Proverbs 15:13 (KJV)

Anyone who follows the PGA knows two things about Matt Kuchar:

1. He walks around the golf course in his comfy Skechers golf shoes.
2. He always has a smile on his face, even when he's not at his best.

Matt is a fan favorite on tour because of his positive attitude and the way he came back from almost losing his PGA card after a slump in the early 2000s.

He rejuvenated himself with a one-plane swing in 2008. Two years later, he was the PGA's leading money winner. He didn't sit back and complain; he made adjustments and improved.

In 2012, he won the Players Championship and moved into the top five in the world rankings. The following year, he defeated Hunter Mahan in the finals to win his first WGC-Accenture Match Play Championship. In Rio de Janeiro at the 2016 Summer Olympics, Matt won the first Olympic bronze medal in golf since the 1904 Summer Olympics.

He has not won a major tournament yet but finished second at the 2017 Open Championship at the Royal Birkdale Golf Club behind Jordan Spieth.

I caught up with Matt on Sunday at The Memorial Tournament in Columbus, Ohio, on his way to the practice tee in 2022.

Normally, I don't bother players on Sunday because they are focused and have a job to do. In a way, I'm walking right into their office. But Matt was coming right at me, so I took advantage of the opportunity. I didn't expect much from him because he was getting ready for the final round.

"Kooch," I said. "I'm writing a devotional book about golf and want to ask you why you always smile, all the time, on the course."

He wasn't expecting that question but stopped to sign a couple of autographs in an area that stated NO AUTO-GRAPHS.

"I've never thought about that," he said. "Why do I smile so much?"

After he signed a couple of flags for patrons, he said, "I think it's just part of my genetic makeup. I feel like I play better when I'm having fun and a good time and that puts me in a good mood. You might as well enjoy yourself while you're out there. I've been blessed and God's been good to me—that's why I smile so much I guess."

Happy is the man that findeth wisdom, and the man that getteth understanding.

—Proverbs 3:13 (KJV)

Tee It Up

What message does your facial expression send to those around you? You may not have a job where it's your responsibility to make twelve-foot putts for a living. But with that also comes pressure. Maybe you hold a factory job or you teach school or you enforce the law. Or maybe you are in college or high school trying to decide what to do in the future. Whatever you do in life, try to maintain a positive attitude with a smile on your face. This may not always be the case, but just like Matt said, "You might as well enjoy yourself while you're out there."

Go for the Green

Life is not always a walk down the eighteenth fairway with a three-shot lead. You might be facing a serious surgery or be bogged down with family issues. Perhaps you face a job loss or health problems. But there are ways to handle difficult situations.

Some suggestions to remind you why you might want to smile during tough times:

1. You are alive. That's the biggest reason of all to smile and be thankful. Be grateful for today because God never promised you tomorrow. If you

waste the day grumbling over things that did not go the way you hoped, that's on you.

2. You are special in the Lord's eyes. Even if you feel alone, God loves you. You have a purpose in life. You might be going through a challenge, but Christ is with you. Your identity is in the Lord and what He has in store for you. All you have to do is obey His will and be willing to be used. "For God so loved the world, that he gave his only begotten Son, that whosoever believeth in him should not perish, but have everlasting life" (John 3:16 KJV).

3. You can inspire and encourage others. No one likes to be around negative people. You can show strength and determination if others see you smile in tough times. "Have not I commanded thee? Be strong and of a good courage; be not afraid, neither be thou dismayed: for the LORD thy God is with thee whithersoever thou goest" (Joshua 1:9 KJV).

4. You will reduce stress. Your body releases endorphins when you smile, even if it's forced. There are studies to prove that you can lift your spirits with a simple smile. "If I say, I will forget my complaint, I will leave off my heaviness, and comfort myself" (Job 9:27 KJV).

5. You are going to heaven. Just to remind you that God wins in the end. You might have a buried ball in the sand bunker with the wind in your face, but if you trust the Lord, you will hole it out for the

win. "Rejoice in the Lord alway: and again I say, Rejoice" (Philippians 4:4 KJV).

Matt finds that when he smiles, he plays better. The same can be applied to you. Smile more and worry less. And in case you don't know who Matt is, watch a tournament on TV. He'll be the one in the Skechers golf shoes and with the great big smile.

Chapter 5

PRIORITIES, PRIORITIES

Rickie Fowler

*And he said to him, "You shall love the Lord your God with
all your heart and with all your soul and with all your mind.
This is the great and first commandment."*

—Matthew 22:37–38

For thirty-six weeks in 2007 and 2008, Rickie was the top-ranked amateur golfer in the world. In 2016, he reached a career-high fourth spot in the Official World Golf Rankings as a professional after he won the Abu Dhabi HSBC Championship.

He's come close in the Majors—tied for second place in the 2014 US Open and 2014 Open Championship, and alone in second place in the 2018 Masters.

The 2010 PGA Rookie of the Year admits he wants to win tournaments, but victory on tour is not the ultimate goal in life.

"When you look at the list of priorities, golf is definitely not at the top of the list," he said. "Winning is nice and important, and I'm sure there are some who think you have to win at all costs. But I'm not one of them. Plenty of people out there don't have the right perspective on life and on work.

"A lot of people think that we as players are supposed to put golf at a higher level and make it number one in life. But there are a lot more things that come first for me. My family. Those close to you. Your health and happiness and life."

The Sunday afternoon I caught up with Rickie at the 2022 Memorial Tournament was not one of his better days on the course. He finished the tournament tied for sixty-fourth at eight over par. I ran into him in the tunnel with his wife and all was well. He didn't win but had his priorities in the right place.

"I know that faith plays a big part in my life," he said. "And I know I don't spend as much time in my faith as I should or would like to, but I think a lot of it. It's important. The values that are taught in the Bible and scriptures about how you treat others. I enjoy it when I'm able to get to chapel and spend time with the guys on tour that are also believers. It's more about who you are and about your faith that gets you through the tough times."

Do not be anxious about anything, but in everything by prayer and supplication with thanksgiving let your requests be made known to God. And the peace of God, which surpasses all understanding, will guard your hearts and your minds in Christ Jesus.

Finally, brothers, whatever is true, whatever is honorable, whatever is just, whatever is pure, whatever is lovely, whatever is commendable, if there is any excellence, if there is anything worthy of praise, think about these things.

—Philippians 4:6–8

Tee It Up

What would you do in this scenario? You've been planning a golf outing with your buddies for weeks. Tee times are difficult to get at this country club, and this is one of your favorites. The tee time is set, and you've been at the range several times and have your swing down to perfection. So you think. You can't wait to try out your new TaylorMade driver or Scotty Cameron putter. The night before, you had your car detailed so you look cool when you pull up to the parking lot. Before you go to bed you check the forecast and it's supposed to be perfect! But during the night, your spouse wakes up and doesn't feel well. Your little one is asleep in the next room and has a big day planned too. When the dawn breaks, your spouse has a fever and cannot get out of bed. Your child wakes up excited about her big day. What do you do? Your spouse needs your help, and you cannot disappoint your child. No one is available to help after you make more than a dozen calls.

Go for the Green

Do you go with your buddies as planned? Do you let your spouse and kid down? You've had this golf outing planned for weeks. But your spouse needs your help. And so does your daughter. Where are your priorities? Would you rather disappoint your buddies or those who are the most important to you? In life, you must make choices like what color shirt to wear or what restaurant to take your family to on a weekend. But when it comes to family, there should never be any doubt about your priorities. And the same goes for the Lord. What is a priority? It's something that is important to you and that you care about deeply. If your faith is important to you, it will show.

Some priorities you should consider having as a man of faith:

1. God. When you put the Lord first, everything else falls into place in life. "But seek first the kingdom of God and his righteousness, and all these things will be added to you" (Matthew 6:33).

2. Family. The family is the cornerstone of the church and the main target of the devil. No one or no circumstance should come between you and your family. There are instances when God understands conflicts, but when you have a choice to make, there is no choice when it comes to your family. If you don't have a spouse or kids, you probably have parents. Take care of them. And take care of yourself too. If you don't take care of yourself, you may not live as long as you hope to.

3. Church. This is a community. This is fellowship. This is friendship. Find a church and get involved. You don't have to be the center of attention or be seen. But do what is needed or what you are good at doing. Go to church on a regular basis and follow His commandment and tithe faithfully. You can't win a golf tournament if you don't tee off on the first tee. Church is your first tee. So go. "So then,

as we have opportunity, let us do good to everyone, and especially to those who are of the household of faith" (Galatians 6:10).

4. Country. You live in the greatest and freest nation on earth that brave men and women fought and died for in order for you to enjoy. Honor your nation and flag and show patriotism.

5. Occupation. Put in an honest day's work for an honest day's pay. No matter what you do in life, do it with a glad heart. If you can pay your bills, you are doing better than most.

When you put these in perspective and in order, there will be no hard decisions to make. Will your life be perfect? A big fat no. But when you put the Lord first, you are more likely to hole that twenty-three footer for birdie on the eighteen.

Chapter 6

LIFE IS MEANT TO BE FUN

Lucas Glover

There is nothing better for a person than that he should eat and drink and find enjoyment in his toil. This also, I saw, is from the hand of God.

—Ecclesiastes 2:24

Winning is not everything. Many well-known athletes and celebrities have unbelievable wealth but are miserable.

You see this in the news often. A movie star or a professional player who has millions of dollars and awards, checks themselves into a rehab or faces legal issues. It happens a lot.

This shows that success as the world designates does not equal happiness.

"Whatever you do has to be fun first if you want to enjoy it," Lucas Glover said. "That's one of the keys to success. You have to want to do it and it has to be fun."

The Clemson University product added he loves to go to work every day. He also admitted it's not always easy. He confessed that being a professional golfer is "very challenging."

"There is an inner drive that has to be there," he said. "You want to do well. We all do. Every struggle is an opportunity to learn and improve. But there has to be confidence and self-belief. Confidence is what it comes down to if you want to do well in golf."

Lucas's biggest victory on the PGA Tour came in 2009 when he won the US Open.

But there were also times when he didn't play up to his potential.

"Taking a break is essential and there were times when I had to take a break," he said. "But I never quit. I just recharged and reset and figured out what I was doing wrong with the swing."

Life is short and is meant to be enjoyed. Christians can have a great time while on their journey that ends here on earth and begins in heaven.

Believers—of all people—have every right to have fun. Do you enjoy your faith?

> *And I commend joy, for man has nothing better under the sun but to eat and drink and be joyful, for this will go with him in his toil through the days of his life that God has given him under the sun.*
>
> —Ecclesiastes 8:15

Tee It Up

Happiness does not come via promotions or big homes, although those are nice if God blesses you in that way. The Christian life is not supposed to be doom and gloom and sorrowful. Life is precious and meant to be enjoyed. We all have moments when tragedy comes along with sadness. But those emotions should be temporary. You can be sad and still have peace in your heart. You can have a spirit of happiness during dark times. This doesn't mean you laugh out loud when the doctor gives you negative news or you find out that you have lost your job. It means the Lord will be with you no matter what happens.

Go for the Green

If you want happiness, the best source of knowledge and wisdom is the Word of God. It's not outdated. It's not old-fashioned or fiction. If you want to be happy and filled with joy and peace, you should read the Bible. I know the author well. He created you and me. He knows your name. That alone should be enough to put a smile on your face and in your heart.

Some keys to real happiness:

1. Gratitude with contentment. Money can't buy happiness. It can bring some fun things into your life but those will disappear or go away. Will you still be happy if that happens? Would you be content if you lost your job or new home? Contentment with what you have combined with godliness is important. When you are content and filled with gratitude, this means you trust the Lord to provide your needs and lead you down the right path. If you are content with what Christ has done for you, that's when you have peace and joy. "But godliness with contentment is great gain, for we brought nothing into the world, and we cannot take anything out of the world" (1 Timothy 6:6–7).

2. Honesty. This is the best and only way to have
   a clear conscience. This might sound obvious to
   a follower of God, but never take it for granted.
   When you are honest with yourself and others,
   you have no reason to feel guilty or self-conscious
   about things. Don't make up a little white lie to
   cover yourself because those will add up and you
   won't be able to keep track of them. Tell the truth.
   Always. "Lying lips are an abomination to the
   LORD, but those who act faithfully are his delight"
   (Proverbs 12:22).

3. Don't compare yourself to others. When you do
   this, you might see the things you don't have
   instead of what you do possess. Never consider
   yourself inferior or superior to others. God made
   you to be you. He does not determine your value
   through what others do in life. The only person
   you must be better than is you—every day.

4. Generosity and charity. Humans by nature are
   self-centered. You want this and that and are never
   satisfied. Material things won't bring you true happiness. This will come when you serve others. And
   this doesn't mean you volunteer or give back one
   day out of 365. You need to strive to make other
   people happy through giving and service. Then,
   happiness will find its way to you. This is why
   Jesus said in Acts 20:35 that "It is more blessed to
   give than to receive."

5. Obedience. If you have kids, you know the feeling
   you get when they do not follow your instruction.

You might be angry or frustrated when you tell your children to do something four or five times. Imagine how the Lord feels when He tells you what to do and you ignore Him or disobey Him. Disobedience is a sin and brings turmoil. It can keep you up at night and invite a bad mood to take over. This might be a small issue like witnessing to a friend or it may be on a larger scale when He tells you to do something in public. He may even be calling you into the ministry or placing another call on your life. Obedience equals happiness.

These are just some suggestions for the keys to true happiness. But if you do not know the Lord, the first step is to accept the gift of salvation. It's free but it cost God His only Son's life. God tells us how to be happy.

Now it's up to you to find it.

Chapter 7

PREPARE YOURSELF WELL

Jack Nicklaus

Whatever you do, work heartily, as for the Lord and not for men, knowing that from the Lord you will receive the inheritance as your reward. You are serving the Lord Christ.
—Colossians 3:23–24

What golf book would be complete without something from Jack Nicklaus?

He is arguably the greatest golfer of my generation and the next several to come.

Jack has a quiet and private faith and prefers it to be personal rather than public. He lets his actions do the talking. He is quiet and even-tempered and philanthropic.

After the Ohio State University product turned pro in 1961, he won more than 70 PGA Tour tournaments, won eighteen Majors, and was named Player of the Year five times. His eighteen Majors, which include The Masters, The US Open, The PGA Championship, and The Open Championship, sometimes called The British Open, may never be topped.

His record stands up there with Cy Young's 749 complete games in the major leagues, Pete Rose's 4,256 career hits, Cal Ripken Jr.'s 2,632 consecutive games played, and of course, Byron Nelson's eleven PGA Tour wins in a row. Many believe those accomplishments will stand forever in the record books.

But the second most impressive statistic is how many times Jack finished second—nineteen—in a Major.

Let that number sink in.

That means he could have won thirty-seven Majors. That's hard to comprehend.

Starting with that 1960 US Open and ending with his eighteenth and final Major championship win at the 1986 Masters, Nicklaus made exactly one hundred Major starts. He only finished outside the Top 10 in thirty-one. Fourteen of those were in 1980 or after. Of the forty Majors played in the 1970s, Nicklaus finished outside the Top 10 just five times.

That's how dominant he was in golf. He was *that* good.

"I don't have a problem with those nineteen second-place finishes," Jack told me in the media center on the grounds of the 2022 Memorial Tournament. "I know I gave a couple of them away, especially the '63 British Open. But that's the game. I looked at those seconds as learning experiences and ways to get better the next time. That's important. I don't like to lose or come in second place. Nobody does. Anyone who knows me knows that I love to win. But that just doesn't happen in this game, and you have to get better."

His attitude about coming in second place is what fueled his success over the years.

"I knew that as long as I properly prepared to do the best and play the best I could, and someone beat me, then well-done on their part," he said. "I never really reflect back on 'what could have been.' I know I played the game at a high level and played it well because I prepared well and played the right way."

Do you prepare each day to defeat the world as a believer of Christ?

> *Do your best to present yourself to God as one approved, a worker who has no need to be ashamed, rightly handling the word of truth.*
>
> —2 Timothy 2:15

Tee It Up

You will have days when you feel like you could knock off Tiger Woods in a longest drive contest. Then the next day you'll experience those moments when it feels like you've quadruple bogeyed the easiest hole on the course. Inconsistency wreaks havoc on the golf course and in life. Answer these questions honestly: Do you go to church faithfully? Do you read the Word of God daily? Do you pray to the Lord every day? Are you prepared? Being a Christian is not a weekend commitment. It's a daily journey.

Go for the Green

Golf is a tough sport to play well. It looks easy, but golf is diabolically difficult. The sport requires mental stamina and extraordinary hand-eye coordination. It's you against the course and requires 100 percent honesty. It will bring jubilation and humility within minutes. And being a Christian looks easy too. You show up to church and smile and shake hands with everyone and toss some money in the offering plate. Simple, right? Not at all. It can bring jubilation and humility within minutes. It requires dedication and commitment and sacrifice. Religion is easy. Following Christ is a daily challenge, but the benefits are more rewarding than any major tournament purse or trophy.

Some ways you can be prepared each day to score and eagle on a life of par-5 holes.

1. Read the Bible every day. This is God's love letter to you. Don't just pick out the short chapters or the verses you like because they make you feel good. Get to know the stories in the Word. Read the Bible all the way through—then do it again, and again. "All Scripture is breathed out by God and profitable for teaching, for reproof, for correction, and for training in righteousness" (2 Timothy 3:16).

2. Talk to God every day. He is always available. God is there when you start your day. He is there when you run into challenges. You can chat with Him in your car on the way to work. Christ likes to hear from you, and He loves it when you thank Him for His blessings to you. Would you go a day without talking to your spouse or significant other, or your kids, if you have any? No. Don't use God as a sounding board and only reach out when you are in the rough or your ball is plugged in a bunker. Talk to Him each day under different circumstances.

3. Be of service every day. This can be done in many ways. A simple smile at work or a thank-you. Buy a cup of coffee for a stranger in line. Let a pedestrian cross in front of you. You also can take a break from work and help someone who is on the streets looking for help. The point here is to have a humble and giving heart.

4. Show gratitude every day. Demonstrate polite manners in a selfish world. Thank God for your food at a restaurant. Gratitude is a lost art. Congratulate a coworker on a job well done and don't worry about you. Lift up others and put your own needs on the back burner. "Oh give thanks to the LORD; call upon his name; make known his deeds among the peoples!" (1 Chronicles 16:8).

5. Attend church often. You cannot win at golf if you don't show up at the course to play. The same goes for you as a Christian. Don't make excuses because you don't go to church as often as you should. If the doors are open, go. If those doors are not open at least twice a week—Sunday and midweek— find another church. "Not neglecting to meet together, as is the habit of some, but encouraging one another, and all the more as you see the Day drawing near" (Hebrews 10:25).

Jack knew the importance of being prepared to play his best and it showed. His record will stand forever.

And if you do these five simple things, you are setting yourself up to be a fantastic follower of Jesus Christ.

Chapter 8

YOU CAN ALWAYS REJOICE

Kevin Streelman

Rejoice in the Lord always; again I will say, rejoice.
—Philippians 4:4

Who wouldn't be happy to get paid to play golf? The pros must, right?

Wrong.

That's one misconception some fans have about players on the PGA, LPGA, and other pro tours. That they get paid to play.

The players, in most cases, must earn a paycheck, much like you and me. Unless a player receives an appearance fee, they must make the cut in each tournament to be financially rewarded. Some have endorsements and incentives in a contract, but most earn their PGA card. And the journey is not as glamorous as some may think.

Along the way, players learn about integrity, honesty, winning, losing, struggling, overcoming, and determination. But through it all, they can have peace during the ups and downs.

In an article about PGA Tour player Kevin Streelman, he was asked his go-to verse for life during times of struggle. Kevin said that he liked 1 Thessalonians 5:16–18 because it encourages him to always be happy. "Rejoice always, pray without ceasing, give thanks in all circumstances; for this is the will of God in Christ Jesus for you."

"To me, this gives us a concise, beautiful way to live life," he said. "Rejoice in God's love. Pray and talk with God constantly. Give thanks regardless of our circumstances. It's easy to be thankful when things are going well, but truly spiritually mature Christians can be thankful when things are getting tough. This is God's secret to living a fruitful, joyous, thankful life. Rejoice, pray, be thankful."

> How beautiful upon the mountains
> 　　are the feet of him who brings good news,
> who publishes peace, who brings good news of happiness,
> 　　who publishes salvation,
> 　　who says to Zion, "Your God reigns."
> The voice of your watchmen—they lift up their voice;
> 　　together they sing for joy;
> for eye to eye they see
> 　　the return of the LORD to Zion.
> Break forth together into singing,
> 　　you waste places of Jerusalem,
> for the LORD has comforted his people;
> 　　he has redeemed Jerusalem.
> The LORD has bared his holy arm
> 　　before the eyes of all the nations,
> and all the ends of the earth shall see
> 　　the salvation of our God.
>
> Depart, depart, go out from there;
> 　　touch no unclean thing;

go out from the midst of her; purify yourselves,
you who bear the vessels of the LORD.

—Isaiah 52:7–12

Tee It Up

Kevin is right when he said that it's easy to be happy and have peace during the good times in life. But sometimes that can also entice you to be content and lead you to feel bulletproof. If you are not careful, you may let your guard down; then the devil will try to slip in and cause havoc. Has this ever happened to you? Or you may ask yourself: How can I be happy and have peace when everything is falling apart around me? Life can have you on the green with a two-inch putt to win the match or deep in the trees with no clear shot to get back in the fairway.

Go for the Green

You will face challenging times. Chances are you have been in battle before and you will see it again. Just because you are a follower of Christ does not mean you will live a stress-free life. But God will give you the grace to face the difficulties. It is natural to grapple and entertain negative feelings during tough situations. But the Lord is the source of all joy and healing. When you connect with God's presence during those struggles, you can find peace in the midst.

Some ways to be joyful and thankful no matter what comes up in life:

1. Focus on the positive. Focus on the Lord and not your circumstances. This does not mean to ignore issues but to trust in the Savior for His deliverance. You don't have to be pleased or happy with what is going on around you, but when you hone in on what Jesus did for you, you can cope better and have peace. When Job lost everything, he still praised the Lord and was later rewarded. "And he said, 'Naked I came from my mother's womb, and naked shall I return. The LORD gave, and the LORD has taken away; blessed be the name of the LORD'" (Job 1:21).

2. Give it to the LORD. Many ask Christ to take away their pain and suffering and wonder why the prayer is not answered. Have you ever thought that maybe you don't want to let it go? That may sound odd, but it may also be accurate. Try this approach. Give it to the Lord and walk away.

> Cast your burden on the LORD,
>   and he will sustain you;
> he will never permit
>   the righteous to be moved. (Psalm 55:22)

3. Go serve others. This serves a couple of purposes—it will get your mind off your problems and will let you see the struggles of others. This will help you gain a new and different perspective. This does not minimize your issues, but it may shed some light on the struggles others face. If you help out at a soup kitchen and feed people who are homeless, you may see your problems in a different

way. And when you do good, it will make you feel better and blessed.

4. Praise the Lord through it all. When you can lift your arms in praise through the storm, imagine how wonderful it will be when the storm subsides. And it will. This will give you strength and encouragement. Don't praise God and expect something in return, praise Him because He is worthy.

5. Never give up. If you follow God's will in your life, you will have peace and joy in your heart. Be resilient and always give the Lord credit and glory. You obtain peace because you have the Lord walking with you—or carrying you—in difficult times. "Therefore do not be anxious about tomorrow, for tomorrow will be anxious for itself. Sufficient for the day is its own trouble" (Matthew 6:34).

Peace and joy are wonderful gifts to accept and keep. But both come through an attitude of rejoicing through it all.

Gratitude and thankfulness will help you realize that rejoicing in the Lord is fun. Try it.

Chapter 9

ENJOY THE GAME OF LIFE

Tracy Hanson

Hate evil, and love good,
*   and establish justice in the gate;*
it may be that the LORD, the God of hosts,
*   will be gracious to the remnant of Joseph.*

—Amos 5:15

I have the classic love/hate relationship with the game of golf.

The love portion comes from the deepest confines of my imagination where I visualize myself hitting each shot perfectly. The hate part comes right after I tee off. I am a typical bogey golfer on a good day.

I'm a true hacker. But a couple of years back, I spent some time with someone who is not. Tracy Hanson was a four-time All-American golfer at San Jose State University and played several years on the LPGA circuit where she banged in seven holes-in-one.

For someone who made a living on the course, Tracy hated the sport. Her hatred for the game was not due to her lousy play, like mine. Her disgust came from another source.

Performance.

She won her first trophy when she was ten. She quickly saw that winning earned her brownie points and approval from her father. Recognition and adoration from her dad fed her desire to play. Tracy continued to win and this provided a false sense of love and acceptance from her father.

The better she performed, the more she won, and the more she was accepted.

Tracy was not addicted to drugs or alcohol or fame. She was enslaved to performance.

Golf was her vehicle, and it landed her a spot on a college golf team. She won eleven individual awards and played on an NCAA national championship team.

But during the long drive to San Jose from her home state of Idaho is where she met the Lord as her Savior. She found comfort in Christ, although she was confused. The person who started the discussion about Christ also was the same person who sexually abused her.

"It was their way to control me," she said. "But I know now that I am a survivor."

She didn't realize the extent of the abuse for nearly two decades because she used the addictive power of performance to mask what had taken place. She needed approval and acceptance, and golf provided that. Doing well on the course and in the classroom numbed the pain she felt from years of exploitation.

"Over time, it got unbearable to the point I could not take it anymore," she said. "I felt shame toward myself."

Toward the twilight of her professional career, her game started to fade.

"I was on a mental and emotional breakdown," she said. "I was working hard on my game and wasn't seeing the results."

No performance meant she had no place to hide from the sexual abuse.

"Everything unraveled," she said. "I lost my joy, my heart, my desire, and I hated golf."

Her challenge, though, was how and when to discuss the abuse. A Christian athlete has standards, she thought.

"I'm not supposed to speak about the bad things in life, only the good things, right?" she said.

She was concerned with public reaction and perception. To help, God sent three women into her life who encouraged her to break the silence and expose the evil and destructive power the shame of abuse had on her life.

After she confronted her past, the chains were broken, and she was set free. She didn't have to perform anymore. God and her friends accepted her as Tracy.

Now her ministry encourages others who may have gone through similar experiences and are held hostage by feelings of shame and guilt.

Sexual abuse is a much-too-common occurrence. According to statistics from the US Department of Justice, only about 30 percent of sexual assault cases are reported. There were 62,939 cases of child sexual assault abuse reported in 2012, and 9.3 percent of maltreatment of children in 2012 was classified as sexual abuse. The National Sexual Violence Resource Center reported that one out of five women will be raped, and one out of seventy-one men will be raped.[1]

If this has happened to you, don't be angry with God. Tracy found the Lord and knows He is the only way to deal with this terrible issue.

If you have ever experienced sexual abuse, know that:

- It's not your fault. Never let anyone tell you that you had it coming. "But if a man find a betrothed damsel in the field, and the man force her, and lie with her: then the man only that lay with her shall die" (Deuteronomy 22:25 KJV).

- You are not alone. God knows pain and suffering and has vowed to carry your load. "And she called the name of the LORD that spake unto her, Thou God seest me: for she said, Have I also here looked after him that seeth me?" (Genesis 16:13 KJV).

- You are important. God proved this when He sacrificed His own Son for you. "For God so loved the world, that he gave his only begotten Son, that whosoever believeth in him should not perish, but have everlasting life" (John 3:16 KJV). YOU MATTER!

Let your steadfast love comfort me according to your promise to your servant.

—Psalm 119:76

---

[1] "Questions and Answers About Sexual Assault and Sexual Offending," US Department of Justice, Dru Sjodin National Sex Offender Public Website, https://www.nsopw.gov/en/SafetyAndEducation/QuestionsAndAnswers.

Tee It Up

Abuse can take many forms: mental, physical, emotional, and sexual. Maybe you have experienced one or a few of these. Remember, it's not your fault. But perhaps you carry some guilt or some responsibility for your feelings. Maybe you have allowed this to distance you from some important people in your life. Perhaps even God.

Go for the Green

Focus on the Family magazine published an article that discussed some general principles from Christian counselors to break the cycle of abuse and to start the process to heal.

A few of the topics and suggestions included:

1. Be honest. Don't allow the devil to put denial in your head. Look in the mirror and tell the truth, especially to yourself. "And you will know the truth, and the truth will set you free" (John 8:32).

2. It's OK to seek professional help. Decades ago, the topic was taboo, and older generations had the perception that seeking help was a form of weakness. There is not a one-stop shop for healing. Trained professionals can assess your situation and make your safety a priority. Healing will not be an overnight stay. Plan on a long haul to victory.

3. Establish boundaries. This helps everyone affected. It's healthy and encouraging to set boundaries.

"Let your speech always be gracious, seasoned with salt, so that you may know how you ought to answer each person" (Colossians 4:6).

4. Seek the Lord. When you spend time with God, don't focus on the why or the how. Be encouraged that He loves you. He wants the best for you, and one day it will all make sense. "Whoever believes in me, as the Scripture has said, 'Out of his heart will flow rivers of living water'" (John 7:38).

5. Forgive. You need to do this because Christ forgave you when you were a sinner. When you forgive, you allow God to heal everyone impacted. Forgive the person who caused you harm and let the Lord deal with everything else.

Chains of sin can be broken. I am a better person for meeting Tracy and hearing her story. She told me she finally enjoys the game because there is no demand to score well with no expectations of bringing home a trophy. It's fun again.

The way it should be.

Chapter 10

WHO DO YOU INFLUENCE?

Jordan Spieth

The fear of the LORD is the beginning of wisdom;
all those who practice it have a good understanding.
His praise endures forever!

—Psalm 111:10

When I was a sportswriter at my local newspaper decades ago, there were four sports legends whom I admired and wanted to meet and interview.

In basketball, Larry Bird.

In baseball, Pete Rose.

In football, Roger Staubach.

In golf, Greg Norman.

I checked all the boxes over the years and was able to spend some time with each one.

Even professional golfers have someone to look up to. Many name Tiger Woods. Others Jack Nicklaus.

For Jordan Spieth, that person is not Woods, Nicklaus, Arnold Palmer, or Bobby Jones. The person he admires is his younger sister Ellie, who is autistic.

Why?

"She's my inspiration," he said. "She is so funny. I really love spending time with her. It is humbling to see her and her friends and the struggles they go through, and which we take for granted. They are the happiest people in the world."

Jordan said Ellie keeps him grounded and humble.

A fan favorite on the course and respected by his colleagues, Jordan's fierce competitive nature is countered with a tender heart for giving back.

"Because of [Ellie] it's always been a priority to me to be in tune to the needs of others," he said.

Soon after he earned a spot in the 2013 Presidents Cup, Jordan started the planning phase of the Jordan Spieth Family Foundation. It brings awareness and financial help to community organizations in four philanthropic groups: special needs for children, military families, junior golf, and pediatric cancer.

"I know it's kind of a lot, but we normally try to give gifts more directly to those in need versus a research-and-development thing. We want to help families who travel, help military families with Christmas, you know just stuff that can make their lives better day to day."

The foundation started small for Jordan but has ballooned into a very large operation that helps so many people and families.

"It's just a part of me," he said. "And my sister is the motivation behind it."

Who do you motivate? What influence do you have on those around you?

Let no one despise you for your youth, but set the believers an example in speech, in conduct, in love, in faith, in purity.
—1 Timothy 4:12

Tee It Up

You may never be a reason why someone starts a charitable foundation, but you can be a source of inspiration. To your spouse. Your children. Your family. Your friends. Your coworkers. Your enemies. You may have heard the comment that you may be the only Bible a nonbeliever reads. This is true. But you also want your actions to speak volumes—louder than words. Will you be an influence for Christ in the workplace and in life in general?

Go for the Green

You can have a major influence on all those listed above. And the best part is you don't have to have won three Majors like Jordan did. And you don't have to have won millions of dollars, although that might be nice. Your attitude and work ethic and how you treat others is worth more than multiple Major wins. It's what people see and experience that matters. And it's what they don't see that helps to mold you into a person of influence.

Some ways you can influence and encourage others to follow Jesus through you:

1. Words. What you say is important. And how you say things goes a long way. Your language needs

to hold honor and not be dignified with what the world thinks is funny. Watch your mouth and what comes out of it. When words leave your lips, you cannot retrieve them. "Let no corrupting talk come out of your mouths, but only such as is good for building up, as fits the occasion, that it may give grace to those who hear" (Ephesians 4:29).

2. Actions. What you do is important. No matter what occupation you have, do it the right way and with integrity and honesty. It's OK to better yourself and be proud of what you do, but make sure it's to glorify the Lord. Your identity does not come from those who pay you, it comes from the One you pray to.

3. Locations. Where you go is important. Let your loved ones see you go to church on a regular basis. Let them see you go to work. Let them see you in wholesome places and never compromise your beliefs on places you visit. "Abstain from every form of evil" (1 Thessalonians 5:22).

4. Hobby. What you do for fun is important. It's OK to let loose occasionally but do it with modesty and integrity. If you have to think twice about if you should take part in something questionable, you should probably choose not to do it. "As for the rich in this present age, charge them not to be haughty, nor to set their hopes on the uncertainty of riches, but on God, who richly provides us with everything to enjoy" (1 Timothy 6:17).

5. Charity. What you do for others is important. Give back to others. This is an area where you don't have to let everyone see. Don't brag about helping others. When you do that, it's not about those you are helping but about you. Be selfless and not a narcissist. Humility will look good on you. "In all things I have shown you that by working hard in this way we must help the weak and remember the words of the Lord Jesus, how he himself said, 'It is more blessed to give than to receive'" (Acts 20:35).

Jordan was influenced and motivated not because of his sister's special needs but rather because of her positive and funny attitude toward life. When you smile and laugh more, your situation may not appear as large as it is in reality. A hearty laugh and a contagious grin can have a tremendous influence on those around you. How YOU treat others and how YOU treat God will encourage and influence more people than you will ever know.

Remember, someone is always watching you.

Chapter 11

A MORAL FOUNDATION

Rickie Fowler

Owe no one anything, except to love each other, for the one who loves another has fulfilled the law. For the commandments, "You shall not commit adultery, You shall not murder, You shall not steal, You shall not covet," and any other commandment, are summed up in this word: "You shall love your neighbor as yourself." Love does no wrong to a neighbor; therefore love is the fulfilling of the law.

—Romans 13:8–10

Everyone wants and needs to love—and to be loved.

It's the core essential desire. Without it, there is no hope and only feelings of abandonment.

First Corinthians 13 describes love as being patient and kind—and that love does not boast and is not arrogant or rude.

There is no place for resentment or irritability, and love rejoices only in truth, the Bible says.

Rickie was blessed to have experienced these emotions, and it allowed him to grow as a man, a husband, and now a father.

"It comes down to providing a good upbringing to my family," he said. "I had it and I want to give it to my daughter.

My parents and my wife's parents were so good to us and provided a good moral foundation."

At an early age he saw the benefits of family values. Telling the truth and working hard were instilled into him as a guide for life.

"I think creating a good foundation for our little one is important and hopefully for any more children we have down the road. I believe it helps to set them up for the rest of their life," he added. "It all starts with us first—the first few years are important to set the tone."

> *Or do you not know that the unrighteous will not inherit the kingdom of God? Do not be deceived: neither the sexually immoral, nor idolaters, nor adulterers, nor men who practice homosexuality, nor thieves, nor the greedy, nor drunkards, nor revilers, nor swindlers will inherit the kingdom of God. And such were some of you. But you were washed, you were sanctified, you were justified in the name of the Lord Jesus Christ and by the Spirit of our God.*
>
> —1 Corinthians 6:9–11

Tee It Up

Are you loved? Do you show love to others? Unconditional love is the best form. I know that I would do anything for my children, even if they go astray. And I would hope they would return the favor. In the worst-case scenario, I can say without a doubt that I will always love them and be there to support them. No matter what. That doesn't mean I would approve of wrong actions, but I'd be there to help them find their way back and encourage them. And above all, love them. But sadly, this is not always the case with everyone.

Go for the Green

You have the opportunity every day to show love and to establish a moral foundation. This can be done for your family, friends, or just for you. If you were given those guidelines as a child, then you're blessed. If you were not, you have the chance now to set a course to show everyone the right way. It doesn't matter if you are a new parent, a newlywed, or a student who has their entire life in front of them. And it doesn't matter if your life is on the sixteenth fairway and you are making the turn into the clubhouse. It's never too late to establish morals.

Some reasons you should always strive for high morality:

1. True happiness. When you demonstrate Christian ethics and do what the Word of God instructs, you will be happy. When you are happy, your mental health is better, and you can handle the stresses of life with a smile. This doesn't mean you won't encounter problems, but it will help you deal with them with hope. "So as to walk in a manner worthy of the Lord, fully pleasing to him: bearing fruit in every good work and increasing in the knowledge of God" (Colossians 1:10).

2. You have a moral road map. If you don't have directions, you will wander aimlessly through life. This will bring out feelings of hopelessness and frus-

tration. You would never tee off in the opposite direction on the golf course. Direction is good. His moral standards for you and me flow from His moral character. He made man in His image because He is good. Good morals provide for a solid foundation. Dive into the Bible and follow His road map for morality. Be holy, truthful, merciful, and forgiving.

3. You will be taken seriously. If you do not live a true life in front of others, you cannot be a source of inspiration. When you have a solid and moral foundation with the Lord, you set the example for others to follow. If you don't walk, others will take note.

4. You will experience a blessed life. Blessings come in all shapes and sizes. And all come because of being obedient to the Lord. If you disobey His will for your life, don't expect to reap the fruits of a good harvest. This also does not disqualify you from hardships and heartaches, but it will help you recognize God's goodness in your life. A clear conscience is one of the best blessings from Christ. "The aim of our charge is love that issues from a pure heart and a good conscience and a sincere faith" (1 Timothy 1:5).

5. You will worry less. When you serve the Lord with all your heart, you can cast your burdens on Him because He cares for you. I know the Bible says in Philippians 4 never to worry, but that can be hard to do 100 percent of the time. When you have a

strong moral compass because Christ lives in your heart, you can take whatever life throws at you. Your faith will be stronger in the end, and you will learn to depend on God for all of your needs. "Anxiety in a man's heart weighs him down, but a good word makes him glad" (Proverbs 12:25).

God lets you know that obedience to Him will not be a burden but rather a blessing. When you set a solid moral foundation because you love the Lord, you will establish a road map for anyone who wants to follow. And it all begins with love.

Love the Lord, love yourself, and love those around you.

Chapter 12

CAN YOU BE USED BY GOD?

Kevin Streelman

In whom we have redemption through his blood, even the forgiveness of sins.
—Colossians 1:14 (KJV)

Everyone makes mistakes. You, me, and everyone else. We all have flaws. We all goof up.

Prisons are full of people who have made wrong choices and paid the price through the legal and justice system. They pay with their freedom and, at times, their lives.

Some get away with it while others live silently with the knowledge they have done wrong. That must be mental torture if the person has any morals or conscience.

Guilt is a powerful tool used by the devil.

And this is not something new. Satan has overpowered the minds of well-intended people to do evil and wrong. He is no match for you and me on an individual basis. He is tricky and sneaky and deadly.

But can you still be used by the Lord after you have confessed your sins?

Kevin Streelman thinks you can, and so should you.

One of his favorite men from the Bible is Paul. Before the apostle met the Lord, Paul was a violent and cruel man.

His only purpose in life was to murder and destroy followers of Christ. His hatred was fueled by evil that came from
the pits of hell. After he became a Christian, Paul went on
to do miraculous works for the Kingdom of Christ.

On his journey, Paul lost his eyesight when the risen
Christ spoke to him about his persecution. Three days
later, his sight was restored, and he was baptized in the
name of the Father. He immediately proclaimed that Jesus
of Nazareth was the Son of God. He wrote fourteen of the
twenty-seven books in the New Testament.

"The fact that God used someone who had actually persecuted Christians and eventually wrote half of the New
Testament, it's a representation of who He can use as broken sinners to do His eternal work," Kevin said.

God will take broken pieces of your life and construct
a loving work of art with your soul and life. It's never too
late, but the sooner you act, the better.

"I wish I would have understood what a relationship
with Jesus was while I was still in school," Kevin said.
"While I went to church and accepted Christ into my life,
it wasn't until my mid-twenties that I truly understood
what an intentional relationship with Jesus looked like."

When you accept the Lord into your heart and ask for
forgiveness, you can start over again, no matter what you
have done.

This does not mean you won't suffer consequences for
past decisions, but it means you can have peace on your
new journey.

You are valuable and can be used for good for God's glory.

Who gave himself for us, that he might redeem us from all iniquity, and purify unto himself a peculiar people, zealous of good works.

—Titus 2:14 (KJV)

Tee It Up

Have you done some things that bring you shame? Do you believe you cannot be forgiven for your past sins? Can you still be used by God somehow? If Christ can use Paul, He can find a way to use you. In case you didn't know, before Paul gave his life to the Lord, he persecuted Christians "beyond measure."

Go for the Green

Never think that you cannot be used by the Lord. It's never too late and you're never beyond redemption. The road may not be smooth and easy, but it can be traveled. You can arrive at your destination. But don't be in a hurry. Redemption may take time. Bridges may need mended and amends can be made.

Some ways you can make sure that your heart is ready for the course include:

1. Be grateful. If you wake up in the morning, that's a great time to begin a day of gratitude. Count your blessings and not what you lack. Focus on the good and the progress you've made. "For all things

are for your sakes, that the abundant grace might through the thanksgiving of many redound to the glory of God" (2 Corinthians 4:15 KJV).

2. Stay honest with yourself. If there is an area where you need to make improvements, ask the Lord for guidance and strength to go forward. Medicine may not taste good going down, but it helps to bring healing. If you have a shortcoming and it's not attractive, recognize it and address the issue with friends and yourself. "He that speaketh truth sheweth forth righteousness: but a false witness deceit" (Proverbs 12:17 KJV).

3. Be aware of your surroundings. Find something positive in each day and let it fuel your willingness to glorify God. "Finally, brethren, whatsoever things are true, whatsoever things are honest, whatsoever things are just, whatsoever things are pure, whatsoever things are lovely, whatsoever things are of good report; if there be any virtue, and if there be any praise, think on these things" (Philippians 4:8 KJV).

4. Be determined. The devil will try to call a penalty stroke on you. Don't fall for his lies. Listen to your caddie (God) and set your sights on victory. "For the word of God is quick, and powerful, and sharper than any twoedged sword, piercing even to the dividing asunder of soul and spirit, and of the joints and marrow, and is a discerner of the thoughts and intents of the heart" (Hebrews 4:12 KJV).

5. Stay focused on the prize. Jesus and heaven are the prize. Focus on the Savior and praise the Lord. "Know ye not that they which run in a race run all, but one receiveth the prize? So run, that ye may obtain" (1 Corinthians 9:24 KJV).

Remember what Kevin said about his relationship with the Lord. "Jesus means everything to me. What He did on the cross bridges the gap between us and God, and eternal life. His teachings are the foundation of my and my family's life. It is my prayer every day to represent Him both on and off the golf course." Kevin is being used—and so can you.

As long as you are honest, grateful, aware, determined, and focused on the Lord, He will take note and use you for His glory.

Chapter 13

HE WILL IRON IT ALL OUT

Stewart Cink

And Jesus answered them, "Have faith in God. Truly, I say to you, whoever says to this mountain, 'Be taken up and thrown into the sea,' and does not doubt in his heart, but believes that what he says will come to pass, it will be done for him. Therefore I tell you, whatever you ask in prayer, believe that you have received it, and it will be yours."

—Mark 11:22–24

A difficult day on the golf course may not mean much to you and me, other than embarrassment in front of your buddies.

But to a professional, it could mean missing a cut and not being paid.

Many believe players on the PGA Tour are millionaires but, in reality, several of them are not. In general, there are about 156 players on the big-boy tour each year. And according to *Golf Digest*, around 100 of them earned $1 million in 2020.

It takes years of practice and sacrifice to make it to the tour. Staying there is another challenge.

Golfers face highs and lows just like everyone else.

"The fact that I am a golfer and have to deal with ups and downs on the course can be a challenge," Stewart Cink said. "Some of those results you cannot control."

Golfers cannot control the weather or the terrain on the course. They cannot control the other players in the group, and in some cases, how fans interact with them.

"That's why my faith in God is so great because it helps me to iron out the highs and lows of my game," he said. "Sometimes, I play great golf and being a Christian—I believe in Christ—and my dependence on Him helps me with keeping life and everything in perspective. The same with the low end. When I'm in a valley if I miss a cut or just can't control the ball, when I'm struggling, my faith keeps me calm. The same thing goes and applies in golf, in life, in marriage, in everything. He irons it all out."

> *If any of you lacks wisdom, let him ask God, who gives gener-ously to all without reproach, and it will be given him. But let him ask in faith, with no doubting, for the one who doubts is like a wave of the sea that is driven and tossed by the wind. For that person must not suppose that he will receive anything from the Lord; he is a double-minded man, unstable in all his ways.*
> —James 1:5–8

Tee It Up

You will experience difficult days throughout life. And you also will have days and weeks of joy and happiness. But how will you act when you slice the ball out of bounds? Perhaps the company you work for is about to announce layoffs. Or maybe your doctor has called you to come into the office ASAP to discuss test results. Life is full of bogeys. How is your faith when you go through a valley?

Go for the Green

Faith is a small word and an easy one to say you possess. But when it's Sunday afternoon and you have a twenty-three-foot putt to win the tournament in front of thousands of fans, will you have the faith you need for victory? Chances are, you will never be in that position. But let's examine a more realistic scenario. The phone rings a few days after a series of medical tests. The voice on the other end says, "We'd like for you to come in tomorrow and go over some of the results with the doctor." I've received that call. That can be, and is, frightening. Your faith may come under attack. How will you respond?

Some ways you can strengthen your faith every day because you should not wait until you need it to have it:

1. Strengthen your faith through praise. When you worship the Lord, through the good and bad, you feel His goodness and stand in His presence. It is then you feel strength and encouragement that He will never leave you.

   A Psalm for giving thanks.
   Make a joyful noise to the LORD, all the earth!
       Serve the LORD with gladness!
       Come into his presence with singing!
   Know that the LORD, he is God!

> It is he who made us, and we are his;
>   we are his people, and the sheep of his pasture.
> Enter his gates with thanksgiving,
>   and his courts with praise!
>   Give thanks to him; bless his name!
> For the LORD is good;
>   his steadfast love endures forever,
>   and his faithfulness to all generations. (Psalm 100)

2. Strengthen your faith through prayer. When you talk with the Lord, thank Him for His blessings and goodness to you. Ask the Father for strength and wisdom and turn over your fears to Him.

3. Strengthen your faith through scripture. Read His love letter to you each day. When you read the Bible on a regular basis, you will see how much God loves you. And everyone has the natural desire to be loved. You can never ever deny His love and adoration for you.

4. Strengthen your faith by witnessing. When you share your story of grace and salvation with others, your faith will increase. A personal testimony will embolden you and give you the confidence you need to surrender your desires to him. "Delight yourself in the LORD, and he will give you the desires of your heart" (Psalm 37:4).

5. Strengthen your faith through acceptance. God's plan is perfect for your life. Things you may not want to take place will have a purpose. You don't

have to understand; just accept. "Nevertheless, not my will, but yours, be done" (Luke 22:42).

When you are able to have the faith in God you need, life will be better. You will have one of the greatest gifts the Lord can offer you: peace of mind.

And that's worth more than the Masters championship.

Chapter 14

DO YOU HAVE COMPASSION?

Cameron Tringale

It is of the LORD's mercies that we are not consumed, because his compassions fail not. They are new every morning: great is thy faithfulness.

—Lamentations 3:22–23

In *Sports Spectrum*, an article discussed how Cameron gives a portion of his tour earnings to fund projects in El Salvador with Compassion International.

He doesn't do this for recognition or for praise and glory but because it's the right thing to do. He feels it's a calling and a worthy cause.

With his gifts, he has had a part in building classrooms and water filters in regions of the nation and has also sponsored a child from Colombia.

I asked him about why he feels compelled to help and give when we spoke after a practice round at the Memorial.

"I am blessed, and I know that from a physical standpoint, a lot of the people and kids there don't know where their next meal is coming from," he said. "They need food and medicine and a lot of them don't know if they will have the medicine they need for themselves or their babies. They depend and lean on God for things that we take for granted. Their faith is remarkable."

He admits he has seen poverty up close and realized how blessed he is through the Lord and wants to give back.

"God has given me so much and He gave me this opportunity to be a blessing to others," Cameron said. "And I know that He wants me to use my resources not for my gain but to pass it along and glorify Him and help others through that. For some reason the Lord has seen fit to bless me and so I want to make sure I praise Him through my giving. I give to help, but I am blessed in return."

He said he was inspired when he saw the faith of those people in El Salvador who have little earthly things but worship the Lord with all they have.

Cameron has earned more than $15 million and gives credit to the Lord by making sure that his charity of choice receives his gift on a regular basis.

How do you show compassion? Do you show any? Do you have any?

> *Thus speaketh the LORD of hosts, saying, Execute true judgment, and shew mercy and compassions every man to his brother:*
>
> *And oppress not the widow, nor the fatherless, the stranger, nor the poor; and let none of you imagine evil against his brother in your heart.*
>
> —Zechariah 7:9–10 (KJV)

Tee It Up

You and I live in a me-centered society. "If it feels good, then do it" has been an anthem that a lot of people have promoted. Social media has glorified self-promotion and invited characteristics of selfishness and narcissism. I'm guilty of it, and if you are honest, you probably are as well to some degree. But are you compassionate toward others? Do you think of those who have less than you? I'm not talking about pity on people. Do you have compassion? It's OK to have possessions if you've worked for them. But do you give back? And if you do, what is your motivation?

Go for the Green

There is nothing wrong with enjoying a good vacation or buying the vehicle of your dreams. But are those things more important than helping your neighbor who struggles financially or a friend who cannot meet their monthly obligations? There is a big difference between charity and a handout to make yourself feel good. God expects you to be a light and an inspiration to others without gloating or bringing it to the attention of others. What would you do if a person approached you on the sidewalk and told you they were hungry? It's easy to keep walking and ignore the problem. When my wife and I were on vacation in California, we were approached by a woman asking for food. By this point, we had been asked for money by several people the night before. But this was different. I took a cold attitude and kept walking. My wife stopped and told the woman that she

would buy something to eat. The woman gladly accepted
the offer, and my wife took her inside a dairy bar for a hot
dog and ice cream. Compassion. My wife demonstrated to
me the art and heart of giving. I learned a lesson.

Some ways you can show compassion to others every day:

1. Be a good listener and empathetic. This is a fantastic way to show compassion. LISTEN to the
   person. Look at their side of the story and don't be
   in a rush to compare your story. You're not trying
   to outdo the person. When you listen, you take an
   interest in what they have to say or how they feel.
   Let them talk and be a support and don't make
   it about you. Empathy is also a form of support.
   You don't have to have had the same experience
   as the person sharing their heart to you, but you
   can try to relate. Let them talk or vent before you
   continue the conversation. Silently ask for wisdom
   from the Lord. "Finally, be ye all of one mind,
   having compassion one of another, love as brethren, be pitiful, be courteous" (1 Peter 3:8 KJV).

2. Be an advocate. Most teams have cheerleaders, and
   all have fans. Get on board and be a cheerleader
   for the person who struggles. When you provide
   encouragement, you give hope and positive motivation.

3. Be a volunteer. This is related to being an advocate
   but goes a step further. When you give your time,
   you donate the most valuable resource you have.

It doesn't cost you anything to help at a nursing home or be a Big Brother / Big Sister. Find an organization or a cause near to your heart. When you become involved in an outreach, you demonstrate compassion for others.

4. Be kind. This one is simple. A smile. Thank you. Politeness. Manners. All of these can brighten someone's day. A kind text to someone going through a trial or a dropped card in the mail can do wonders. "He that followeth after righteousness and mercy findeth life, righteousness, and honour" (Proverbs 21:21 KJV).

5. Be quiet. Never seek attention or recognition for your actions. If others find out, it might inspire them to do the same. But don't brag or post selfies of you at the Salvation Army or soup kitchen. Self-promotion defeats the purpose and makes it about you. And never talk about the person to others and gossip. "Let nothing be done through strife or vainglory; but in lowliness of mind let each esteem other better than themselves" (Philippians 2:3 KJV).

When Cameron saw the needs of those in El Salvador, God spoke to his heart and revealed compassion. Compassion toward others is a cornerstone of being a Christian. When you do what you can for Christ, everyone involved is blessed. The organization, if there is one. The recipient is blessed. You are blessed. And God is glorified.

What else is there that's more important?

Chapter 15

DO YOU WANT MORE OF GOD IN YOUR LIFE?

Jack Nicklaus

O God, you are my God; earnestly I seek you;
  my soul thirsts for you;
my flesh faints for you,
  as in a dry and weary land where there is no water.
                                    —Psalm 63:1

The greatest golfer in the history of the sport has accolades no one else will ever achieve.

After Jack Nicklaus's first year on the PGA Tour in 1962, he won the PGA Rookie of the Year award—a sign of many great things to come.

He won the PGA Player of the Year five times and sat atop the PGA Tour money list eight times. Over his career, he won the Bob Jones Award and the Payne Stewart Award and countless others.

His likeness is featured on a commemorative issued five-pound note by the Royal Bank of Scotland, which made him the first living person outside of the royal family to appear on a British banknote.

In 2001, Jack was honored with the Lombardi Award of Excellence from the Vince Lombardi Cancer Foundation.

The award was created to honor the Green Bay Packers football coach's legacy and is awarded annually to an individual who exemplifies the spirit of Coach Lombardi.

He was even chosen and given the rare privilege to "dot the i" in "Script Ohio" during a Buckeye's football game on homecoming on October 28, 2006. That is considered the highest honor a nonband member can receive at Ohio State University. Not many nonband members have been selected to "dot the i." He was the fifth person ever selected for the honor. Others included Bob Hope and Woody Hayes.

Jack was named a Global Ambassador for the International Golf Federation in 2008 and played a major role in bringing golf to the Olympics in 2016 and 2020. On May 19, 2014, he was awarded the Congressional Gold Medal in recognition of his attitude of good sportsmanship.

He holds the record for most Major wins—eighteen—and is third on the all-time wins list with seventy-three.

These are just the tip of the iceberg when it comes to Jack's accomplishments.

"I love to compete, and I love to win," Jack said. "No one likes to lose. But I've never reflected back on my career. I don't mean that in an arrogant way. I played the game well at a high level because I love competition. It makes everyone better."

He said golf has been good to him and his family for the past seven decades.

"No other sport can do what golf has done for me," he said. "I respect the game. All of what has happened has been amazing, but it has never exceeded my expectations.

I am blessed but I always want more, and I always want to do better."

How much of God do you want? Do you do more for the Lord?

> *Seek the* Lord *while he may be found;*
>   *call upon him while he is near;*
> *let the wicked forsake his way,*
>   *and the unrighteous man his thoughts;*
> *let him return to the* Lord, *that he may have compassion on him,*
>   *and to our God, for he will abundantly pardon.*

—Isaiah 55:6–7

Tee It Up

Maybe you have done well throughout your life. You've been recognized in the community and in your church for your kindness and dedication within the area. Perhaps you belong to some civic organization and have donated countless hours of your time to help those less fortunate than you. Perhaps you have achieved greatness in the workplace and have everyone's highest regards in your area of expertise. Now let's look at life from a spiritual perspective. What have you done for the Lord? He is not looking for titles and accomplishments. Those are great to receive for hard work, but Christ is interested in what's in your heart and not what is on display in your trophy case.

Go for the Green

Your attitude and desire to seek more of God can only come from you. No trophies or plaques on your shelves or walls can bring you the satisfaction that only comes from serving the Lord. Jack said he always wanted to do more and do better on the course. Do you entertain that same outlook when it comes to your faith and being a follower of Christ?

Some ways you can get closer to God to find out what He can offer you:

1. Admire His creation. Slow down and see what you are missing in life. You are pulled in many different directions, and that entices you to neglect your priorities, including your time alone with God. Take a few moments to gaze up at the stars at night or listen to children laugh. Admire the flowers and the countryside. Thank Him for His blessings and allowing you to enjoy His creation. "The heavens declare the glory of God, and the sky above proclaims his handiwork" (Psalm 19:1).

2. Watch what you watch. You need to guard your heart from evil, and part of that is guarding your eyes. Movies that promote things you should not see, along with TV shows and the internet, are traps to bring you down. If you are not careful, the toxic images and messages will slip into your heart and thoughts. It can pollute your mind. Be careful what you watch, especially offensive images and shows.

> I will not set before my eyes
>   anything that is worthless.

> I hate the work of those who fall away;
> it shall not cling to me. (Psalm 101:3)

3. Fast to get closer. This should never be used as a bargaining chip or a way to influence God to give you what you want. Instead, fasting is a method and practice to draw closer to God and for Him to reveal His plans for you. Fasting is not just sacrificing a meal or two. It's all about sacrifice in general. Maybe give up golf for a few weekends. Give up distractions, such as your cell phone for a while so you can get in tune with Christ.

4. Forgive. Forgive those who have caused you harm even if they do not ask. Jesus commands this from you, and it's also a wonderful way to show your love for Him via obedience. Ask the Lord to bless those who have caused you pain or suffering. Then ask Jesus to change your heart and attitude toward that person. Never hold a grudge or become bitter. "And whenever you stand praying, forgive, if you have anything against anyone, so that your Father also who is in heaven may forgive you your trespasses" (Mark 11:25).

5. Write it down. Journal about what the Lord has done for you. This will help you remember His grace and mercies toward you. Go back and see what prayers He answered. You will develop an attitude of gratitude and appreciation for His love for you. "Bless the LORD, O my soul, and forget not all his benefits (Psalm 103:2).

These are just some suggestions to help you win in your journey of faith. Jack said it best when he said he loves to win. He also said, "No other sport can do what golf has done for me." Try this one: "No other God can do what the Lord has done for me."

Always want more of Him.

Chapter 16

FELLOWSHIP IS A KEY TO CHRISTIAN SUCCESS

Stewart Cink

Therefore encourage one another and build one another up, just as you are doing.

—1 Thessalonians 5:11

Community is key in any relationship. Not just any community, but one that encourages and inspires strength and growth.

I've written a few other devotionals and each one has a common theme. Community.

In *Dugout Devotions: Inspirational Hits from MLB's Best*, two coaches I interviewed had similarities.

Mike Matheny, then-manager of the St. Louis Cardinals, and Clint Hurdle, then-manager for the Pittsburgh Pirates, both have a personal "board of directors" they meet with on a regular basis.

And it's not a business meeting. It's a personal accountability gathering. Clint calls his group his "Mount Rushmore" of friends while Mike refers to the group as a personal board of directors.

These two men of faith have the groups to hold them accountable and to learn on the journey of life.

Stewart Cink sees the value of this too.

"Out here, we have a great group of guys who go to chapel and the fellowship is amazing," he said. "They are huge influences in my life. My wife is also strong, and she helps me tremendously. She encourages and supports me and is a great role model. Over the years, I have had a lot of people shaping me . . . Jesus would not let me go."

You and I need this too. Fellowship makes the journey enjoyable. But you must realize the huge difference between accountability and judgment. Accountability is great, and needed, but be careful not to slip into judgment.

When you hold someone accountable or responsible for actions or words, you assure that the person will be evaluated on his or her performance or behavior and own up to what they do or say.

When you pass judgment, you allow your opinion to come into play and you compare the actions or words to a level that you determine. You decide what the person did or said, right or wrong, when you judge.

Somewhere along the way, Christians have fallen into the trap of casting judgment instead of promoting accountability.

Remember, only Christ can and will judge. But you can be held accountable and help to hold others to the same standard.

Iron sharpens iron, and one man sharpens another.
—Proverbs 27:17

Tee It Up

Do you have issues with being held to a higher standard or held responsible for your actions or words? If you have a job, you have expectations and responsibilities to your employer, right? What will happen if you fall short in meeting your goals? You'll be let go or given a chance to make improvements and adjustments. Do you help others along the journey to be better? I've read many articles about teammates and competitors of Boston Celtics legend Larry Bird and how he made everyone around him a better player. Are you that kind of a person?

Go for the Green

One of the most beneficial things you can do for your spiritual growth is to form your own Christian accountability group. It does not have to be large. It can be three or four people you trust. And it also should include those who may not agree with you on all issues. You don't want a group of rubber stampers. You need different opinions, but people with the same overall philosophy. That means you don't want to include nonbelievers. This group will be formed so you can share your faith, struggles, successes, and dreams.

Some ways having an accountability group can help you and those involved:

1. It will help you stay focused. In today's fast-paced society, it's easy to get sidetracked. When you meet with your group, either in person or on the

phone or by Zoom, you can be encouraged and also offer motivation. When you have to answer for your actions or words, you'll find it more difficult to stray from the path God paved for you. "Follow the pattern of the sound words that you have heard from me, in the faith and love that are in Christ Jesus" (2 Timothy 1:13).

2. You will grow in your faith. When you share your struggles and challenges with someone close to you, it opens the door for them to pray for you. When you grow closer in your relationship, your accountability group will learn more about what it means to follow the Lord. "For though by this time you ought to be teachers, you need someone to teach you again the basic principles of the oracles of God. You need milk, not solid food, for everyone who lives on milk is unskilled in the word of righteousness, since he is a child. But solid food is for the mature, for those who have their powers of discernment trained by constant practice to distinguish good from evil" (Hebrews 5:12–14).

3. You will be encouraged in the tough times. You will face struggles not only on the course but in life. When you don't know where to turn for help, those people close to you can offer words of encouragement and prayers. This can be of great comfort. And in turn, you can do the same for others when they face difficult times. "Be strong and courageous. Do not fear or be in dread of them, for it is the LORD your God who goes with

you. He will not leave you or forsake you" (Deuteronomy 31:6).

4. You will be held to a higher standard. When you drive a car on a highway, you will encounter signs to help you navigate to your destination. Without them, you may get off on the wrong path. These groups can help steer you in the right direction. If you plan to go somewhere you shouldn't, someone in your group should tell you it's not a good idea. They want you to succeed. They don't want you to stumble.

5. You will be motivated. You can bounce ideas off each other and brainstorm while you try to figure out God's plan. Not only will you grow, but when others toss in opinions, doors can open to things you never thought of before. "Beloved, we are God's children now, and what we will be has not yet appeared; but we know that when he appears we shall be like him, because we shall see him as he is" (1 John 3:2).

Moses had Aaron and David had Nathan. Clint and Mike have their groups. Stewart looks to his wife and the fellow believers on tour for inspiration. Accountability partners will be a blessing to you. And you can do the same for them.

You can help one another overcome temptations and stay on the right course.

Chapter 17

YOU MUST WANT MORE

Bubba Watson

So as to walk in a manner worthy of the Lord, fully pleasing to him: bearing fruit in every good work and increasing in the knowledge of God.

—Colossians 1:10

Although you and I are born into sin, I believe everyone has a desire to do good. Many people will make unfortunate choices and find themselves in the mud and mire of sin. But a big part of human nature is to please and be a good person.

Little kids want approval from parents, and they want to earn that smile from their coaches and teachers.

Bubba Watson was the same way as a kid who grew up in Bagdad, Florida.

He said in an article that he considered himself a good guy.

"Didn't cuss, didn't cheat, didn't steal, didn't lie, didn't drink, didn't do drugs," he said. "I was doing the right things, but I didn't know what that meant."

He searched for approval. Just like you and I do, or did, from the Lord. During his senior year in high school, two girls who lived in his neighborhood invited him to a church youth group outing.

"After a few times going, I realized this is what I wanted to do," he said. "This is truth here. And I gave myself to the Lord."

He went to play golf at the University of Georgia where his commitment to God became solidified. There he started to date former WNBA player Angie Ball, and the couple attended church together.

That is where and when the two knew they wanted to follow Christ together. "We started turning to the Lord for our decisions," he said.

The Watsons are a true Power Couple for God. They have adopted two children and want to be positive role models for them and everyone else who sees their lifestyle.

Bubba, who was given the nickname by his father after former NFL great Bubba Smith, is well-known for his driving distance and trick shots. He has won two Majors and has finished atop the driving distance stats five times.

He strives to make a good living with golf but wants to be known for his faith more.

Let the word of Christ dwell in you richly, teaching and admonishing one another in all wisdom, singing psalms and hymns and spiritual songs, with thankfulness in your hearts to God.
—Colossians 3:16

Tee It Up

Maybe you are like Bubba. You're a good person. You play by the rules. You don't cuss, cheat, steal, lie, drink, or do drugs. That's fantastic and you should be commended.

You have admirable morality and are an upstanding person. But are you a Christian? Have you given your heart to the Lord? Or perhaps you are a believer who has been in a slump recently. That does happen. Golfers call it a funk. Do you have times when Christ does not seem close and things are not going well in life?

Go for the Green

If you have not given your life to Christ, then you are lost and without hope. If you are a follower of Christ, are you in need of a birdie from above? You may be a good person. The kind of person any parent would want to date their child. Or you may be a fantastic example of a community leader and the best employee anyone could ask for. But do you long for something else? Do you want to be accepted? Do you want to live for God or have Him closer to you?

Some ways you can find yourself close to Jesus right away:

1. Make new connections. Step back and look at the people in your circle. Are they a positive influence on you or a negative one? Perhaps it's time to surround yourself with like-minded people. You may be hanging out with the most popular person, but what is the cost? "Do not be deceived: 'Bad company ruins good morals'" (1 Corinthians 15:33).

2. Listen and be quiet. There might be times when you can't hear what God is telling you because you talk too much. You might be trying to talk

yourself into something the Lord doesn't want you to do. Cleanse yourself from the noisy surroundings and meditate on God. Consider a fast to draw closer to seek direction and guidance. "Know this, my beloved brothers: let every person be quick to hear, slow to speak, slow to anger" (James 1:19).

3. Soak in His creation. Maybe it's time to take a break and see all the wonders the Lord has created. Go see the Grand Canyon or the ocean and marvel at His works. If you don't have time, stand or sit in your backyard at night and look up at the universe. Appreciate His creativity and stand amazed. "By faith we understand that the universe was created by the word of God, so that what is seen was not made out of things that are visible" (Hebrews 11:3).

4. Be of service. "If you are waiting on God, do what waiters do . . . serve." I love this. I am all about service to others. When you do this for the right reason, you put your life in perspective. You can volunteer to help those less fortunate than you or you can simply be a light in your workplace. Service to others doesn't always mean charity. It means to do for others with no expectation in return.

5. Pray and praise. You can ask God into your heart, and you can also praise Him for all His blessings on you. The Lord wants your praise and adoration. He created you and sent His Son to die on the cross for your sins. Thank Him for that. "For

God so loved the world, that he gave his only Son,
that whoever believes in him should not perish but
have eternal life" (John 3:16).

It doesn't matter if you are a good person or one who has
strayed. You can find what you are looking for on your
knees in prayer. He is there, and He has the answers.

Just ask for help and guidance.

Chapter 18

KEEP THE RIGHT COMPANY

Scottie Scheffler

Fulfill my joy by being like-minded, having the same love, being of one accord, of one mind. Let nothing be done through selfish ambition or conceit, but in lowliness of mind let each esteem others better than himself.
—Philippians 2:2–3 (NKJV)

When Scottie chose a caddie, the most trusted source of knowledge and confidence for a professional golfer to lean on, one qualification topped the job description: he wanted a fellow believer in Christ to walk next to him on the course.

In *Sports Spectrum*, Scottie stated how much he relied on caddie Ted Scott, who carried the bag for Bubba Watson for more than ten years.

"He keeps things loose," Scheffler said. "We have a lot of fun together. I respect him a lot as a person, and I respect his work ethic as a caddie. And so, for me, it's been a pretty easy relationship so far just because I respect him so much."[2]

---

[2] Joshua Doering, "Scottie Scheffler Staying Grounded in Faith During Rise to Golf's World No. 1," *Sports Spectrum*, April 8, 2022, https://sportsspectrum.com/sport/golf/2022/04/08/scottie-scheffler-grounded-faith-world-number-1/.

It didn't take much time for the duo, who met in Bible study on tour, to capture the WM Phoenix Open in February 2022. Soon after the win, Scottie went to Instagram where he gave praise to God.

"Overwhelmed at getting my first PGA Tour win," he stated on the social media platform. "So thankful to the Lord, our families and friends, and everyone else apart of the team. An unbelievable experience we will never forget. Let's do it again!"[3]

And they did.

Three weeks later the two won the Arnold Palmer Invitational in Orlando, Florida, by one stroke.

Three weeks after that, Scottie and Ted captured the WGC-Dell Technologies Match Play in Texas.

With that win, Scottie moved to the number-1 spot in the Official World Golf Ranking.

In April, Scottie won his first Major, The Masters in Augusta, Georgia, by three strokes and became the fifth golfer to enter the tournament ranked number 1 and go on to win.

In an interview with PGATour.com, he said it's important to be with people who share similar beliefs.

"I'm a Christian guy, so that's important to me," he said. "But even if you're not a Christian, life is important to spend with people you enjoy. If you don't have close, quality friends, I don't think whatever you're doing is

---

[3] Scottie Scheffler (scottie.scheffler), "Overwhelmed at getting my first PGA Tour win," Instagram, February 15, 2022, https://www.instagram.com/p/CaBWiWOlwYe/.

important. So that would be my most important advice to someone. Find something you enjoy doing and enjoy doing it with other people."[4]

In his first six starts of the 2022 season, Scottie won four tournaments. At season's end, he was named the 2022 PGA Tour Player of the Year and won the Jack Nicklaus Award.

What a year!

Better yet—Scottie and Ted—what a professional team.

Let each of you look out not only for his own interests, but also for the interests of others.
—Philippians 2:4 (NKJV)

Tee It Up

How do you choose your friends? Are your decisions inspired by popularity or by similar attractions and interests? Of those people you call friends, how many of them do you really trust? Do they encourage you? Do they inspire you? Do they make you feel important? If you should put those questions on paper next to a list of your "friends," how many would make the cut?

Go for the Green

As renowned columnist Walter Winchell popularized: "A real friend is one who walks in when the rest of the world

---

[4] Zephyr Melton and Kevin Prise, "100 Questions with Scottie Scheffler," PGATour.com, September 18, 2019, https://www.pgatour.com/korn-ferry-tour/news/2019/09/18/100-questions-with-scottie-scheffler.html.

walks out." How true. It's OK to have acquaintances and colleagues who are friendly toward you, and you to them. You have people in your life and in your community whom you know well. You see the same people at the grocery store or even at church. You smile and laugh then go separate ways. That's part of life. But how many "true" friends do you have? Is being a Christian the first standard you look for in a friend?

Some reasons why you should choose those friends who are Christians:

1. A friend will pray for you. This is the best characteristic of a friend. And I don't mean a person you pass at the store who says "I'll pray for you" and walks away. Find a person who will put a hand on your shoulder and take your issues to the Lord in prayer while you are with him or her. When you and a friend can talk to God together, there is a special bond. "Behold, how good and how pleasant it is for brethren to dwell together in unity!" (Psalm 133:1 NKJV).

2. A friend will give good advice. Understand the difference between giving advice and direction. A good friend will express his or her side about an issue and let you make your decision. That kind of friend can be a guide and a person you can consult with confidence. Someone who is not a friend will give you an order and expect you to abide by that command.

3. A friend will hold you accountable. And they will expect the same from you too. If you get off track and start down a wrong road, a friend will wave the flag and point you toward the right path. People use a GPS to make sure they arrive at their destination without getting lost. There may be several intersections at one point, but the voice in the box will guide you through the mess. That's what a friend will do.

> For if they fall, one will lift up his companion.
> But woe to him who is alone when he falls,
> for he has no one to help him up. (Ecclesiastes 4:10 NKJV)

4. A friend will encourage you. Everyone needs encouragement. Even those who give it all the time. Community and feelings of acceptance are important. Little acts you may find insignificant can make someone's day. A friend should notice when you are down or discouraged. A simple text or call or hug can go a long way. "For I long to see you, that I may impart to you some spiritual gift, so that you may be established—that is, that I may be encouraged together with you by the mutual faith both of you and me" (Romans 1:11–12 NKJV).

5. A friend will have your back. When others walk away, the true friend will be there. You may have done something that offends others, maybe even your friends. But a friend will let you know that and still stick by you. They may even help you with any recovery or restitution you may have to

make. And they will also be there in tough times, such as a job loss or a bad breakup. "A man who has friends must himself be friendly. But there is a friend who sticks closer than a brother" (Proverbs 18:24 NKJV).

Scottie thought it was important enough to have a Christian by his side for his work. And that is crucial. When you choose a friend, a colleague, a mate—put a like-minded believer at the top of the list.

Chapter 19

HOW ARE YOU DEFINED?

Scott Stallings

In whom we have boldness and access with confidence through our faith in him.

—Ephesians 3:12

Scott Stallings is a household name to those who follow professional golf. That is why many fans try to snag an autograph when they see him on the practice green or walking from the clubhouse. Some may even wait by his car in the parking lot, which is not advised.

His first few years on tour were not easy. In 2009, he missed the PGA Tour's Qualifying School by one stroke. He landed on the Nationwide Tour where he made the cut in nineteen of the twenty-eight events. Two years later he earned his card to play with the big boys.

That also was a challenge for the first few weeks. He missed the first five cuts before he finished tied for forty-second at the Puerto Rico Open.

In July, he won the Greenbrier Classic in West Virginia for his first win on tour. He took home the honor after he won in a three-way playoff against Bob Estes and Billy Haas. He won his second tournament in 2012 at the True

South Classic and his third at the Farmers Insurance Open two years later.

His ups and downs on tour have helped to create a never-give-up attitude, but it does not define him as a person. He lets his faith in Christ do that for him.

"I know that my score on the course doesn't define who I am," he said in an interview with FCA. "I'm thankful for where God has placed me at this time in my life. Every day I wake up and thank Him for the opportunity He's given me to let His light shine through me, and I pray that will always be the case."[5]

Years ago a poll revealed that 63 percent of people who call themselves American also call themselves Christian. That number has dropped to just above 50 percent in recent years.

But what is a Christian?

Webster says a Christian is "one who professes belief in the teachings of Jesus Christ." In its adjective form, it means "of or relating to Christianity." It has its origins in the Greek *christianos*.[6]

God's Word says a Christian is a follower of Jesus Christ. That is cut and dry and doesn't leave any room for doubt.

How are you defined?

If someone had one word to describe you, what would that word be? Maybe *hardworking, loving, caring, funny,*

[5] "Scott Stallings, PGA Tour," *FCA Magazine,* May 1, 2012,
   https://www.fca.org/fca-in-action/2012/05/01/scott-stallings-pga-tour.
[6] Merriam-Webster online, s.v., "Christian," noun,
   https://www.merriam-webster.com/dictionary/Christian.

punctual. Or perhaps the word would not be as flattering. Words like *liar, thief, jerk, nasty, unfriendly,* or *selfish* might come out of their mouth.

> *For we are his workmanship, created in Christ Jesus for good works, which God prepared beforehand, that we should walk in them.*
>
> —Ephesians 2:10

Tee It Up

If your pastor were to go to your place of business and take a poll of what your colleagues thought about you in one word, would you be afraid of what may come out of their mouths? Or what if he went to your golfing buddies and asked the same question, what would they say? Do you turn in a correct scorecard, or do you forget a stroke here and there? Or how about those who live with you or who have had business dealings with you in the past? Have you used unkind words in front of people? Have you horn-cussed a motorist who cut you off?

Go for the Green

There are many words that could describe you. How would you describe yourself with one word? During a job interview, I always hated it when the interviewer asked, "How would your last boss rate you?" I didn't like that question because I didn't want to brag or boast about myself. But this isn't what you are going for. This is about your reputation or testimony. If you stay consistent in your beliefs and your character, then maybe these five words will be used to define you by everyone:

1. Saved. This sums it up. If you have given your heart to the Lord and follow Him and His teachings, you are on your way to heaven, and no one can change that. That is a terrific word to describe you. Does everyone know this about you? "And they said, 'Believe in the Lord Jesus, and you will be saved, you and your household.'" (Acts 16:31).

2. Compassionate. This can come about through donating your time and energy to help those who are less fortunate than you. If you give your time and money to help, you are doing God's work on earth. Does everyone know this about you? "Be kind to one another, tenderhearted, forgiving one another, as God in Christ forgave you" (Ephesians 4:32).

3. Dedicated. Do you show up for work on time? Do you give an honest day's work for an honest day's pay? Do you make the special person in your life feel that way? Do you honor your promises and your word? Does everyone feel this way about you?

4. Honest. Do you walk the walk and talk the talk? Do you back up what you say? Do you hold true to your convictions? Only you know this. "Better is a poor person who walks in his integrity than one who is crooked in speech and is a fool" (Proverbs 19:1).

5. Faithful. Do you read your Bible and pray every day? Do you attend God's house and worship on a regular basis? Do you tithe 10 percent or more? Do you testify and give a witness to God's goodness in your life? Does everyone see this side of you? "One who is faithful in a very little is also faithful in much, and one who is dishonest in a very little is also dishonest in much" (Luke 16:10).

No one is perfect. On the golf course, Scott has enjoyed good days and suffered through the tough ones. But he is known as a professional golfer and defined as a man of faith.

What you do will define you and leave a testimony for people to describe you. Make them good words.

Chapter 20

WHAT CHOICE DO YOU HAVE?

Cameron Tringale

For whatever was written in former days was written for our instruction, that through endurance and through the encouragement of the Scriptures we might have hope.

—Romans 15:4

Even professional golfers have bad days on the course.

I covered a practice round a few years ago at the Memorial Tournament. On the back nine, I watched one of the top golfers in the world chunk a second shot on a par five. I couldn't believe it. The ball went about twenty yards, and the divot went about ten.

He was embarrassed, laughed, and looked up at the heavens. What else could he do?

I've been there more times than I want to admit, but I don't play golf for a living. For you and me, chunking a shot happens on a frequent basis. For some spectators, the player's flub made him more relatable to hackers.

But for pro golfers on tour, a mishit like that happens maybe two times in a decade.

But it happened.

When the tournament finished, this golfer finished in the top 10.

He persevered and put the bad shot behind him. After all, that's what practice is for—to get the kinks out.

"What other choices do you have but to keep going when things go bad for you?" Tringale said. And for the record, he is not the golfer who chucked the ball. "You can either keep going and pray and read the Word and try to learn. Or you can wallow in despair and feel bad for yourself. I've done both, especially in this game of golf, but I try to lean on the former and just expect each day and realize the Lord has a purpose for you."

The golfer who hit the terrible shot in practice years ago either went to the practice range or just put the blunder behind him later that day. Or both.

"What seems to be a struggle or a failure in life, there is something to be learned and that constantly changes. I seem to learn a lot more from those mistakes," Tringale said. "I learn more from the tough times than the good times. I enjoy the good times and learn from the struggles."

I have fought the good fight, I have finished the race, I have kept the faith.

—2 Timothy 4:7

Tee It Up

Life has tougher challenges than chunking a ball on the back nine on a practice round. But you probably have days when you look up at the heavens and shrug and laugh. Maybe you react differently. Perhaps you scream or take things out on other people or your friendly and dedicated pet at home. Perhaps you are faced with life-changing decisions and are frustrated to the max. Or maybe you find yourself in the woods and near the out-of-bounds markers with no shot at the green. What choices do you have? You can take your clubs and walk off the course and quit, or you can head to the range and figure out your swing.

Go for the Green

Determination is tough. It takes a lot of hard work and discipline. Just like the game of golf, life looks easy. But when it comes down to the fundamentals, you realize golf is a tough game to play well. Life has the same characteristics. It can appear to be fun and easy, but the sand traps can leave you bewildered and confused. You can hit the best tee shot in the world, but it can land in a divot and leave you with an extremely difficult second shot to the green. Sometimes life is not fair. But you must adjust and be determined to hit the green in regulation. Golfers are creatures of habit.

Some habits to pick up to keep you focused and determined to make the cut:

1. Feed your faith. You cannot grow unless you eat. That's true in life and in golf. Each player who does well on tour must practice and make sure he or she is doing what is needed to become better and stronger. You can feed your faith by going to church on a regular basis, by reading the Word of God daily, by praying at least once a day if not

more. If you slack off on any of these, the devil
will spot the weakness and cause you to chunk a
shot or miss the gimme putt. "Man shall not live
by bread alone, but by every word that comes from
the mouth of God" (Matthew 4:4).

2. Claim the promises. Your faith is yours alone.
It's your responsibility. You cannot count on the
faith of your pastor or spouse, although they can
be supporters. When a golfer hits a fantastic shot
near the cup, it's because of their swing. The caddie may have had some input, but the player exe-
cuted the swing. The Lord has promised you many
things, but it's up to you to claim them. "And we
know that for those who love God all things work
together for good, for those who are called according to his purpose" (Romans 8:28).

3. Think right. What dominates your thoughts?
What is on your mind most of the time? Work?
Family? Children? Your spouse? Vacations? Golf?
Those are all OK. But where the mind goes, so does
the spirit. Your thoughts influence your words and
actions. They should feature happiness, peace, joy,
and other fun things. "We destroy arguments and
every lofty opinion raised against the knowledge
of God, and take every thought captive to obey
Christ" (2 Corinthians 10:5).

4. Praise God often. Don't just go through the
motions to make God happy. He knows where you
are sincere. When you glorify God in church or in
the confines of your room, He is pleased. When

you can worship and praise God in tough times, you will become stronger and appreciate the blessings. Strong Christians have a correlation between praise and worship and happiness and peace. It works. "Give thanks to the Lord, for he is good, for his steadfast love endures forever" (Psalm 136:1).

5. Chuck your baggage. This can be a variety of things that might include depression, discouragement, stress, unconfessed sin, unforgiveness, and addiction. If something holds you down, give it to the Lord to toss into the pond. Seek professional help or talk with your pastors. It's OK to do that. This will help you make that twelve-foot putt for birdie and enjoy life more.

Cameron posed a great question when he asked what choice do you have but to keep going? It's a rhetorical question. Determination and endurance are vital in your walk of faith. There will be times of turmoil and doubt. But the way to keep going is to develop strong habits that will assist you along the way and help you become stronger. It doesn't happen overnight.

Good habits are a must to help you win in the end.

Chapter 21

KNOW WHAT IS TRULY IMPORTANT

Jordan Spieth

And he said to him, "You shall love the Lord your God with all your heart and with all your soul and with all your mind. This is the great and first commandment."
—Matthew 22:37–38

Jordan Spieth, the Dallas, Texas, native burst onto the scene in 2012 and grabbed the attention of players and fans across the nation. His golden-boy image combined with his killer instinct on the course made him a fan favorite.

By the time he was twenty-two years old, he had pocketed a total of $23 million through his winnings on the golf course.

Jordan reached the number-1 player in the world rankings in 2015 and held on to that for twenty-six weeks.

But, like many golfers, he slid into a funk and a slump and struggled to win and, at times, make some cuts. But he was OK.

He still drew a large crowd at tournaments because people could not help rooting for him. He's likable. No drama. No foul language. No tantrums. Just class and true sportsmanship.

When Jordan plays in the field, he is a legitimate contender to win every time. That doesn't always happen, but he shows up and gives the game and fans his all.

It's no secret he holds his faith in high regard and makes no apologies for that.

"For me, it's my faith, then my family and then, after that, this is what I love to do," he said. "As long as I keep those priorities that way, I'm happy and blessed."

> *Do not be anxious about anything, but in everything by prayer and supplication with thanksgiving let your requests be made known to God. And the peace of God, which surpasses all understanding, will guard your hearts and your minds in Christ Jesus.*
>
> *Finally, brothers, whatever is true, whatever is honorable, whatever is just, whatever is pure, whatever is lovely, whatever is commendable, if there is any excellence, if there is anything worthy of praise, think about these things.*
>
> —Philippians 4:6–8

Tee It Up

Today, more than ever, life is busy. Do you have any memories of times when you were not so busy? If you are old enough, you may recall simpler times when life wasn't hectic. Is there a lot of demand for your time today? How are your priorities? You must be aggressive to make it in today's world. The job market is competitive and there is so much competition at all levels. Do you find it tough to find time for God? Do you dedicate time for the Lord each day? Do your priorities have your faith first?

Go for the Green

If your day is like mine, from the time you wake up until you lie down to go to sleep, time flies by. Every day can be a blur. Sometimes that is good, but other times it can be a drag on your spiritual health. The world and the devil will do all they can to lure you away from the goodness of God. It's easy to get wrapped up in life and drift from your faith. "I'll read my Bible and pray tomorrow" is the attitude Satan wants you to possess. He will toss things in your way to make you procrastinate.

Some ways you can prioritize your faith:

1. Commit. When a golfer commits to a shot, he or she feels more confident. If they don't do that, the ball goes through the air without clear direction. As a Christian, you must commit to faith. After all, you have a relationship with the Lord. You can't expect to be a good weekend golfer if you don't practice. A commitment takes work. Every relationship needs attention. Take time every day to honor Christ. "Commit your way to the LORD; trust in him, and he will act" (Psalm 37:5).

2. Schedule. You know that God is there all the time, but are you there? If you make a tee time with your buddies, you show up on time. If you punch a time card at work, you show up on time. Do the same as a follower of Christ. Select a time that works for you because Jesus is always available. Don't waiver or make excuses. Life happens, but make sure you

keep your date with the Lord every day to either read His letter to you or pray. If you need to put a reminder in your phone, then do it. Make your daily tee time with the Lord.

3. Community. If you are like me, you don't like to play golf by yourself. It's just more fun to play with your friends, kids, or a spouse. The same goes for your walk with the Lord. When you have some people to worship with or meet for a Bible study, it makes it more enjoyable. Rides are more fun with people you love or like. Make sure you surround yourself with people who will help you. If you don't have a four-some, then find one. Community is important for growth. "For where two or three are gathered in my name, there am I among them" (Matthew 18:20).

4. Attitude. The reason fans love Jordan is because he is genuine and sincere. He doesn't have a fake personality and he always tries his best. That's what you must do on your journey with the Lord. Be honest. Be real. Be willing to be used by God. Be humble. Be grateful. Attitude—not image—is everything. "Humble yourselves before the Lord, and he will exalt you" (James 4:10).

5. Worship. This can be your way to praise God for all He has done and will do for you. It can be in many forms. Raised arms. Hand claps. Bowed head. Open hands. Bent knee. Praise Him the way you feel you can praise Him. But do it every day and every night. "Praise the LORD! Praise God in his sanctuary; praise him in his mighty heavens!" (Psalm 150:1).

When your faith comes first, everything else in life will follow. You cannot put your work, your friends, or golf in front of God.

When you prioritize faith and family first, you put yourself in a good position for a major win.

Chapter 22

TELL EVERYONE ABOUT YOUR VICTORY

Scottie Scheffler

But in your hearts honor Christ the Lord as holy, always being prepared to make a defense to anyone who asks you for a reason for the hope that is in you; yet do it with gentleness and respect.
—1 Peter 3:15

Kurt Warner led the St. Louis Rams to a Super Bowl XXXIV title in 2000 and thanked his Savior, Jesus Christ, on live television for millions to see and hear. Nine years later when his Arizona Cardinals won the NFC championship to advance to another Super Bowl, he told Terry Bradshaw the same thing. He praised God and thanked the Savior for His blessings for millions to see and hear again.

Kurt has admitted that when he professed Jesus Christ from the podium, that was one of the greatest ways to witness to the world that he is a Christian. It promoted and encouraged accountability. He said, after he made those statements, that "everyone knows about my faith."

When Scottie Scheffler won the Masters in 2022, he followed Kurt's path. After his victory earned him the coveted green jacket, he told the international and national media gathered why he plays professional golf.

"The reason why I play golf is I'm trying to glorify God and all that He's done in my life," Scheffler said. "So for me, my identity isn't a golf score. Like Meredith [his wife] told me this morning, 'If you win this golf tournament today, if you lose this golf tournament by 10 shots, if you never win another golf tournament again,' she goes, 'I'm still going to love you, you're still going to be the same person, Jesus loves you and nothing changes.' All I'm trying to do is glorify God and that's why I'm here and that's why I'm in [this] position."[7]

Scottie's boldness and willingness to share with millions why he plays will embolden him to live his faith every day with more determination.

Now the world knows he is a follower of Christ. This is important because now everyone knows he is an ambassador for the Lord.

He does not want to tarnish God's image and wants to show the world the love Christ has for him.

Proclaiming the kingdom of God and teaching about the Lord Jesus Christ with all boldness and without hindrance.

—Acts 28:31

---

[7] Michael Ryan, "Scottie Scheffler Wears His Christian Faith on His Sleeve as He Dons the Green Jacket for His First Masters Tournament Win," The Lion, April 11, 2022, https://readlion.com/2022/04/11/scottie-scheffler-wears-his-christian-faith-on-his-sleeve-as-he-dons-the-green-jacket-for-his-first-masters-tournament-win/#:~:text=Long%20before%20he%20donned%20the,Christian%20faith%20on%20his%20sleeve.

Tee It Up

Have you ever found yourself in a situation where you have had the chance to proclaim the gospel for several people to hear? Maybe you have had the opportunity to speak in front of some people or have been asked to explain why you've been successful at work. It doesn't have to be in front of dozens of people. Maybe your buddies at work want to know why you pray before your lunch or why you smile often. These moments can intimidate but may not come around a lot either. Will you take advantage of those times? What would you do if given the platform to proclaim your salvation in front of a crowd?

Go for the Green

An opportunity to profess Christ can present itself in different ways. You want to be careful to represent your Savior in a wonderful light, and you don't want to turn off people with a brazen attitude. You want to tell others how good the Lord has been to you. Have you ever seen a "street corner preacher" who says good things but condemns everyone who walks by? They have the right intention, but their delivery and approach may put forth a negative persona. There are ways you can share your faith with others and help encourage them to do the same.

1. Testify in church or Sunday school. Just a few simple words of gratitude will do. When you share your personal account of how God has touched

your life and blessed you, it will have an impact on someone. No one can take away your own experience. Always be thankful and avoid any negative words. When you do this, you let those in attendance know you trust the Lord with your life. "Therefore do not be ashamed of the testimony about our Lord, nor of me his prisoner, but share in suffering for the gospel by the power of God" (2 Timothy 1:8).

2. Take to social media. This will allow those who follow you on platforms to be aware of your faith. Be careful not to drive your followers away either. It's OK to have followers who do not profess a faith. You can be a witness to them. Mix up your shares and posts to include scripture, encouraging quotes, and, my personal favorites, pictures of food and desserts. You also can put words in your profile that tell followers that you love the Lord. Bubba Watson's profile says he is a "Christian. Husband. Daddy. Pro Golfer. Underwear model #urwelcome." He covers all the bases there and maybe a tad bit of TMI with some humor. "Let your speech always be gracious, seasoned with salt, so that you may know how you ought to answer each person" (Colossians 4:6).

3. Organize or attend a Bible study. Scottie and his caddie, Ted Scott, met at Bible study on the PGA Tour. When you gather with like-minded people, it will encourage and inspire you to be bolder with your profession of faith.

4. Be confident. When Scottie was given the chance to tell the world about his Savior, he did it with honesty and class. He explained in short detail why he plays golf. His objective in everything he does is to bring glory to God. When you are given the chance to share your faith, take it and don't back down. Show love and genuine gratitude. Scottie does it with golf. You can do it with whatever job you have too. "Whoever trusts in his own mind is a fool, but he who walks in wisdom will be delivered" (Proverbs 28:26).

5. Use good judgment. There is always time to tell others about the Lord, but do it in a way not to antagonize others. You want to be bold and have a sense of urgency because time is fading, but you always want to be sensitive to the Holy Spirit. Pray and ask the Father to open doors for you to share your faith. He will provide.

The chances of you winning the Masters or the Super Bowl and having a microphone put in your face for millions to hear or see may be low. But whenever you are presented with an opportunity to proclaim your faith, will you be ready? You don't have to be in front of the media to do this.

Be prepared and enjoy giving your message of hope to two, three, or even fifty people.

Chapter 23

YOU JUST NEVER KNOW

Payne Stewart

Because, if you confess with your mouth that Jesus is Lord and believe in your heart that God raised him from the dead, you will be saved.

—Romans 10:9

Payne Stewart's reputation in the early 1990s was that of a snooty golfer who rarely spoke to the media in a kind manner. He seldom signed autographs, if ever, in his younger days. He didn't like the distractions that accompany being an iconic sports figure.

On the course, he possessed one of the smoothest golf swings ever. He was also considered one of the best-dressed players on tour and wore his infamous "knickers" and ties.

On this particular day, Payne triple-putted the eighteenth green and stormed off to sign his scorecard. He didn't talk to the media. He didn't sign autographs or communicate with anyone.

That's how he was then. Many thought of him as a spoiled brat.

I read that he grew up in a Christian home, but Payne never proclaimed a faith.

But after he won his third Major tournament, the 1999 US Open Championship at Pinehurst Resort in North Carolina, with a one-stroke win over Phil Mickelson, fans noticed and saw a different Payne.

The year before, he lost the same tournament in devastating fashion. But a year later, he won. When he accepted his trophy, he gave credit to someone he had never recognized in the past.

"First of all, I have to give thanks to the Lord," he said. "If it weren't for the faith that I have in him, I wouldn't have been able to have the faith that I had in myself on the golf course."

He went on to say, "I'm proud of the fact that my faith in God is so much stronger, and I'm so much more at peace with myself than I've ever been in my life."[8]

Incredible. Humility. Gratitude.

That's not the Payne Stewart I encountered. Somewhere between his first Major win and his last, he found God.

In an article, Payne's mother admitted she saw the change in her son.

"Payne talks more with God now," his mother Bee was quoted. "He's a different man, a better son. He talks more with journalists and autograph seekers, whom he used to regard as lower life forms."

---

[8] Christin Ditchfield, based on the book by Tracey Stewart with Ken Abraham, "Payne Stewart: A Changed Heart," https://vietchristian.com/gospel/heart.asp.

When the change happened, people noticed. They also noticed he was one of the first athletes to wear the WWJD bracelet.

In 1999, a few months after he won The US Open, Payne tragically died in an airplane crash near Mina, South Dakota.

This is how Payne described himself prior to his death: "I'm not a Bible-thumper—I can't get up there on a rock and tell you what it all means because I don't know. But I'm learning, and I like what I'm learning," he said.

Then he was killed.

Thank God he left a testimony.

Therefore do not be ashamed of the testimony about our Lord, nor of me his prisoner, but share in suffering for the gospel by the power of God.

—2 Timothy 1:8

Tee It Up

Have you put off making a profession of faith? Are you waiting until you are older to turn your life over to the Lord? Do you believe you have all the time in the world to make that decision? What are you waiting for? You read about the change in personality Payne had. After he started to win, his demeanor changed. He was nicer. He was more kind. He was different and his fans noticed and liked the change. Then he died. He was in the prime of his life. Why do you wait?

Go for the Green

People put off saying yes to Christ for a lot of reasons. The biggest is because the devil does not want you to live for the Lord. He wants to destroy you and make sure you spend eternity with him in hell. He will tell you a bunch of lies to keep you from giving your heart to the Lord. If you want to make the best decision in your life to be a Christian, you may run into these mistruths from Satan.

1. You are not ready. If you have thought about it, you are indeed ready. You know it's the right decision. But the devil is telling you to wait. Just think of where Payne would be today if he waited. "But concerning that day and hour no one knows, not even the angels of heaven, nor the Son, but the Father only" (Matthew 24:36)

2. You are not worthy. No one is worthy. But when you accept His gift of salvation, the Lord allows you to tee off on the first hole again. You start anew and he tosses your sin into the sea of forgetfulness. You have worth because Jesus died for you. "I have been crucified with Christ. It is no longer I who live, but Christ who lives in me. And the life I now live in the flesh I live by faith in the Son of God, who loved me and gave himself for me" (Galatians 2:20).

3. Life will not be fun. The Christian life is a blast. You can enjoy a clear conscience and kindness

every day. Laughter is common and honesty and integrity are the norm. Christians have fun—good clean fun. "There is nothing better for a person than that he should eat and drink and find enjoyment in his toil. This also, I saw, is from the hand of God" (Ecclesiastes 2:24).

4. Everyone goes to heaven anyway. Only those who have given their heart to the Lord and have had their sins washed in the blood of Jesus will enter heaven. God does not send anyone to hell. He gives you a choice where to spend eternity. "In my Father's house are many rooms. If it were not so, would I have told you that I go to prepare a place for you?" (John 14:2).

5. It's too complicated. This is where people make things more difficult than they are. The devil tosses in different doctrines and rules that muddy the water. Just remember that God sent His only Son to die on the cross for your sins and to rise three days later in victory. He has a place prepared for those who follow Him. It's that simple. "The unfolding of your words gives light; it imparts understanding to the simple" (Psalm 119:130).

Putting off the decision to become a Christian can be costly. Listen to your caddy. In this case, the Holy Spirit. God stands waiting for you to ask Him for forgiveness. But He won't force you to make the decision.

You must be the one to commit. Don't wait.

Chapter 24

SOMETHING NEW

Jack Nicklaus

Therefore, if anyone is in Christ, he is a new creation. The old has passed away; behold, the new has come.
—2 Corinthians 5:17

The Memorial Tournament is commonly referred to as the unofficial fifth Major on the PGA Tour. Players make a point to add it to their schedule because they all want to win "Jack's Tournament."

The tournament was founded by Nicklaus in 1976 and is played on a course he designed: Muirfield Village Golf Club in Dublin, Ohio, a northern suburb of Columbus. Muirfield Village is a large neighborhood that erected a bronze sculpture of Jack in the middle of Muirfield Drive.

In 1966 Nicklaus won his third Masters and a whopping $20,000, big money at that time. After that win, he had the vision for the Memorial.

"I was talking to some (club) members, and I knew what a great tournament this was at the Masters," he told me in Dublin. "And I thought to myself, what a great idea to bring something like this to Ohio. That is where it all started."

Jack looked at property and stumbled onto the grounds that are now home to his tournament.

At the time, the biggest events around Columbus were the six home games of the Ohio State Buckeyes football team.

"There were no professional sports around here except the AAA team in Columbus," Nicklaus said. "So, we came up with the idea of memorializing great players of the past and focus it around the time of Memorial Day."

Jack wanted the tournament to give back to organizations that benefit needy adults and children. Today, the primary beneficiary of the tournament is Nationwide Children's Hospital—a relationship that spans more than four decades—in Columbus. But other charities receive contributions from the event too.

"Each year the tournament brings in the best of the best players," Nicklaus said. "We have a great field. The main goal will always be to give back to the area. And to think this all started with a dream and a vision."

And though your beginning was small, your latter days will be very great.

—Job 8:7

Tee It Up

Do you want a new start? Something fresh? Do you have a desire to be more and do more in Christ? Or maybe you want to enjoy God's blessings but have never experienced His forgiveness. Maybe you are stuck in the sand bunker and feel you don't have a clear shot at the green. Perhaps you think your life is like a golf ball lying in a divot and you don't have a way to make solid contact. Or maybe you think you can never start over. You are wrong and putting limits on God.

Go for the Green

If you are a new creation in Christ, the old has passed away and a new day has arrived. If you are one of God's children and He has forgiven you, you *can* start over whether you think you can or not. When the Lord hands you the 6 iron and tells you to trust your swing and go for the green, don't second-guess Him. It doesn't matter if you've been fired or lost a relationship, you can start anew with Christ. When you commit to the Lord, you can have a new everything.

Some items He can make new:

1. A new relationship. You are no longer separated or alienated from the Lord. You have the closest relationship you could ever want. You are a new creature in Christ. Everything is new and clean and pure.
2. A new purpose in life. You may hold an important position at work and that's fantastic. But in the end, it doesn't matter. When you enter into a relationship with Jesus, you now have a real purpose. You no longer have to drift through life wondering about your worth. You are important and your life has meaning. Just ask Him for direction. "I cry out to God Most High, to God who fulfills his purpose for me" (Psalm 57:2).
3. A new journey. Your old ways are gone. You have a new direction to go. When you commit to a new

journey and a life as a believer, your life has just started. You will encounter problems on this journey, but you also will experience love and compassion. "But for you who fear my name, the sun of righteousness shall rise with healing in its wings. You shall go out leaping like calves from the stall" (Malachi 4:2).

4. A new destiny. You can do anything you want, if that is what God has in store for you. Destiny also means obedience and when you follow His will for your life, your destiny will be more than you ever imagined. "Do not be conformed to this world, but be transformed by the renewal of your mind, that by testing you may discern what is the will of God, what is good and acceptable and perfect" (Romans 12:2).

5. A new power. Now you have God to call on—and not just in times of troubles. He is a friend and Father who can do all. He is your heavenly Father and wants what is best for you all the time. In His promises, He says He will never leave you and will instill in you His Holy Spirit to help. "Finally, be strong in the Lord and in the strength of his might" (Ephesians 6:10).

Jack had the inspiration to begin a new journey when he saw the vision for The Memorial Tournament. You can allow God to set you toward a new destination.

Only He can provide you with a new relationship, a new purpose, a new journey, a new destiny, and a new power.

Chapter 25

BE OK WITH HIS TIMING

Sam Burns

Wait patiently for the Lord.
Be brave and courageous.
Yes, wait patiently for the Lord.

—Psalm 27:14 (NLT)

I hate to wait. I have little patience. Just ask my wife. She cannot surprise me at Christmas because I possess a nasty habit of unwrapping and rewrapping the gifts addressed to me under the tree. I must admit, I'm good at this sneaky craft and it helps me cope with holiday anxiety.

My justification? I want to plan my reaction in case I don't like the gift.

But I will demonstrate patience when I'm a few miles out in the Gulf of Mexico fishing for sharks or grouper. The waiting game is well worth the time when a big one ends up on the hook and later lands on the dinner plate.

But when the topic becomes winning a tournament as a professional golfer, waiting should be written in the job description.

Sam Burns, who turned pro in 2017, has won a few tournaments. If he had it his way, he would hold up a trophy each week he played.

But that's not reality.

He's patient. He puts his faith in Christ for all things—even his tour wins.

"I think just knowing that my timeline isn't always best or my timing isn't always right means I'm not always going to win," he said. "So if I don't win, I can be OK with that. If I do win, I give Him the glory."

You and I live in an "instant" society.

We want our food fast. We want our internet fast. We want news now. We all want instant gratification. We buzz around the golf course in a cart because it makes the round go by even faster.

That could make having faith and trust even more difficult to master. If you get used to things happening fast, how will you be able to trust the Lord?

"Just being able to trust and really deep down believe that His timing is perfect—and obviously at times it's frustrating because you want things to happen—and His plan is perfect gives me patience," Burns said.

The game of golf oozes patience. To walk eighteen holes usually takes me about three or four hours. Sometimes it takes four if I include a mulligan per hole.

How are you when it comes to waiting on God? Does He move too slow for your liking?

I wait quietly before God, for my victory comes from him.
                                                —Psalm 62:1 (NLT)

Tee It Up

To wait on the Lord means waiting with expectation and hope. It means believing that God hears your prayers and will answer or reward you for seeking His will. But what if the answer is no? It happens. Have you ever wanted the Lord to answer your prayer *now*? Maybe you were presented with your dream job, and they wanted an answer immediately. But you didn't have peace and asked for more time to make your decision. Perhaps you have a personal dilemma, and you want to act as soon as possible. Could it be a trap set for you from the devil? Maybe. In my life, if I am pressured to give an answer to something and I'm not given time to consider it or talk it over with my spouse and pray about the circumstance, the answer is *always* no. Except if I'm asked if I want free bacon and coffee, the answer is a very fast *yes*!

Go for the Green

Remember when the Israelites sinned against God because they did not recall the good things He did for them in the wilderness? You should also remember the great things He has done for you in the past. Maybe you have a loved one suffering from health issues. It's hard to wait and it makes you feel helpless. At times, the only thing you can do is wait. That is when God has done His best work. If you rush into something, be ready for the hasty consequences. When it's difficult to wait on the Lord, no matter the situation, consider the benefits of waiting on His plan.

1. Waiting will humble you. The Lord wants you to depend on Him. He will encourage you to wait to show you that you cannot have it your way all the time. Life is not Burger King. The longer you wait and trust His plan for your life, the more you will recognize the answer to your prayer is not about you. It's about giving God the glory for everything. "But if we look forward to something we don't have yet, we must wait patiently and confidently" (Romans 8:25 NLT).

2. Waiting will keep you from fake blessings. The devil wants nothing more than to lead you astray and have you blame God. Satan will create fake blessings so you don't receive what the Lord wants you to have. If it sounds too good, chances are it is. The devil will make everything look fabulous and then will pull the rug out from under you after you make a hasty decision. Wait on the Lord to reveal the right decision to you. "Listen to my voice in the morning, LORD. Each morning I bring my requests to you and wait expectantly" (Psalm 5:3 NLT).

3. Waiting will reveal your real motive. Why do you want something in the first place? God is not a cruel and stingy Father. If you have kids and they ask for items in the store, do you give it to them? They want something because it looks appealing, and it will change their life forever, right? Wrong. When you wait, the Lord will see your real reason. If you ask and He agrees, then it will happen in His time.

4. Waiting will renew your strength. Scripture tells you that if you wait upon the Lord, He will renew your strength like an eagle. In fall 2019 and into early 2020, I was ready to open my own business. I looked at some "perfect" locations, had the perfect business name, and could obtain the financing and had "the plan." It was a sure bet. But nothing happened. No one returned calls and the dream fizzled out. I gave up. I was frustrated. Shortly after, COVID-19 hit and many businesses in the area closed. If I had gone ahead of God and forced the business to happen, it would not have lasted. His plan was safer than mine.

5. Waiting will make the answer more wonderful. When the answer does come and it's the way you envisioned or prayed for, then it's a joyous time. When you finally land that job or close on the perfect home, you feel blessed and have a peace about you that only comes from God. The same will happen when you enter heaven. You must wait. You must endure. "I say to myself, 'The Lord is my inheritance; therefore, I will hope in him!'" (Lamentations 3:24 NLT).

When you wait, you cultivate and build strength needed to be a victorious Christian. God made the process of giving birth nine months for a reason. The waiting process culminates in the miraculous birth of life.

It's precious. It's indescribable. It's a joy. Wait.

Chapter 26

TELL EVERYONE IN EVERY WAY

Bubba Watson

In the same way, let your light shine before others, so that they may see your good works and give glory to your Father who is in heaven.

—Matthew 5:16

New York Yankees slugger Aaron Judge uses his enormous Twitter account to let everyone know he is a follower of Christ. Not only does he have scripture on his profile, but he puts the word *Christian* as his first description, followed by faith, family, and then baseball.

Bubba Watson does a similar thing. *Christian* is the first word, followed by husband, daddy, pro-golfer. That is followed by a questionable "underwear model" salutation. Scary, but funny.

Bubba said by using Twitter to encourage people, he wants his followers to know that God is his first love.

In an article, he said, "For me, it's just showing the Light. There's people who want to put down Christians. I try to tell them Jesus loves you. It's just a way to be strong in my faith."[9]

---

[9] "Faith Down to a Tee," New Life Publishing, https://www.newlifepublishing.co.uk/latest-articles/ib-art/faith-down-to-a-tee/.

He spreads his tweets around and shows a lot of family pics and some with other sports celebrities he runs into. But occasionally, Bubba will share a Bible verse.

Social media is a powerful tool that can be used for fun and to encourage.

Bubba went on to say he doesn't allow haters to deter him from sharing the Word of God or ruin his day. He draws spiritual strength by letting his followers know he is a believer.

In addition to his Twitter posts, Bubba has made a few humorous appearances in videos by Christian artists. He was in the video "Michael Jackson," made by Christian hip-hop artist Andy Mineo, and was also featured in the song "Ima Just Do It" by KB, another Christian artist.

He likes to have fun, play some golf, and let everyone know that his faith is the most important thing in his life.

But in your hearts honor Christ the Lord as holy, always being prepared to make a defense to anyone who asks you for a reason for the hope that is in you; yet do it with gentleness and respect.
—1 Peter 3:15

Tee It Up

Are you ready to tell your followers and friends you are a Christian? Do they even know? Maybe you are in an environment where you might be punished if you display a Bible on your desk in your office. You may find yourself at lunch with colleagues who use foul and vulgar language. Do you have it in you to make a bold statement and let those around you know you are a Christian? Be smart and cautious and avoid a physical confrontation because the world is full of violent people who have short fuses. Would some people be surprised if they found out you are a Christian? Not everyone can win the Masters like Bubba and have the clout to catch the attention of followers when they scroll Twitter or Facebook or Instagram. You don't have to have a green jacket to tell others about the Savior.

Go for the Green

Make it a priority to let the world—or at least your friends and family—know you are a child of the King. The same way Bubba does. You can show that you are a normal person who loves the Lord with all your heart.

Some suggestions on how to send a clear message:

1. Be friendly. When you extend a kind word to whomever you meet, that leaves an impact. A simple smile might invite people to hear about your testimony. If you show an enthusiastic attitude and smile, some might want to know about the motivation behind your mood. Be prepared to tell them that your sins are forgiven and that you are on your way to heaven. "So that in the coming ages he might show the immeasurable riches of his grace in kindness toward us in Christ Jesus" (Ephesians 2:7).

2. Pray over your meals. You may be the only Bible a person sees that day. When you bow your head and pray over a meal at a restaurant, it may send a message you are grateful and thankful that God

has blessed you with food for strength. It may be a small gesture, but it could have a huge impact.

3. Use social media. Bubba lets his followers know he is a Christian in his profile. You can do the same. And all your posts don't have to be spiritual. But avoid posting things that will damage your reputation. Post about the Lord, animals, funny quotes, and of course, plenty of food pics.

4. Be consistent and support your church. Show up at your church for regular services as well as special occasions. If you invite someone to church and they come and you're not there, that sends a negative message. There are times when you cannot, and God understands. For Bubba, he hopes to be playing for a championship on Sundays, but he still goes to chapel. "So faith comes from hearing, and hearing through the word of Christ" (Romans 10:17).

5. Don't back down. Never let anyone deter you from showing everyone your love for God. If someone is offended, let them be offended. It's not worth missing heaven to make a person who judges you more comfortable. Stand your ground. "Not that we are sufficient in ourselves to claim anything as coming from us, but our sufficiency is from God" (2 Corinthians 3:5).

Not everyone can hit a golf ball a gazillion yards like Bubba or be a master of trick shots like him, but you can send a message to all who can travel around the world in one click that you are a Christian.

Chapter 27

THE LEGACY

Corey Pavin

We will not hide them from their children,
but tell to the coming generation
the glorious deeds of the LORD, and his might,
and the wonders that he has done.

—Psalm 78:4

Some plays throughout history stand out more than others, moments that are forever etched in memories. Good or bad, those seconds last an eternity.

Remember David Tyree's remarkable helmet catch in the Super Bowl?

New York Giants quarterback Eli Manning somehow escaped three New England Patriots pass rushers and heaved a pass downfield in the final two minutes of Super Bowl XLII.

Tyree jumped up with a defender on him and pressed the ball against his helmet as he went to the turf to secure the thirty-two-yard pass play. The Giants went on to score a touchdown and win 17–14.

NFL films dubbed it as "The Play of the Decade." It was also Tyree's final touchdown catch of his career.

In the NBA playoffs in 1981, Larry Bird hit a shot that will never be duplicated. "Larry Legend" took a shot at the right side of the T and knew it was off the moment it left his hand.

His basketball instinct knew where the ball would come off the rim, and he darted toward the baseline. When the ball rebounded off the rim, Bird caught the ball in the air, switched hands from his right to his left and put the shot back for the bucket before his feet hit the floor. And, his body was behind the backboard when the ball snapped the net.

The difficulty level of this shot is simply off the charts.

Corey Pavin is also remembered for a golf shot that will forever define his ability under pressure.

In 1995, at the US Open at Shinnecock Hills Golf Club in New York, Corey sealed the deal on the final hole for the win.

He entered Sunday down three strokes to Greg Norman and Tom Lehman.

But on the seventy-second hole, he launched a 228-yard approach shot with a 4 wood that landed five feet from the cup. He sank the putt for par to secure the only Major win of his career.

Four years before that, Corey gave his heart to Christ. Although he was a young Christian at the time, he knew not to have expectations as a believer.

"That doesn't mean you're going to be a better golfer," he said about his faith. "My faith is who I am, that's what I do with my life, it's private and personal."

Although he won fifteen tour events and was the 1991 Player of the Year on the PGA Tour, he will always be remembered for that one spectacular shot that earned him the title of US Open Champion.

What will you be remembered for?

One generation shall commend your works to another, and shall declare your mighty acts.

—Psalm 145:4

Tee It Up

When you graduate high school or college, you want to earn a living and enjoy success. There is nothing wrong with that. But what else do you want to achieve? Do you want to be noted for the person who spent sixty hours a week at the office? Do you want to be remembered for being the life of the party? Or do you wish that your legacy be determined by how much golf you played while your kids grew up?

Go for the Green

Your legacy will go on long after you have departed this world and entered heaven's country club. It will be remembered for your wins and losses. It will be remembered for your made putts as well as your chunked second shots. The good and the bad will linger in the minds of those you were close with in life. What effort do you put in to make sure your legacy is positive?

Some ways you can be remembered when you enter the clubhouse for the final time:

1. For being there. Make sure you are present for the moments in life with those you love. When it comes time to sign your scorecard, you want those people you cherish to be there. You never want to be remembered as the person who was a workaholic. Attend events with your kids and visit your parents before they depart. Be there. For everything.

2. For your generosity. You can't take your Taylor-Made clubs with you. Saving money is fine, but hoarding it is not a good quality. Find causes to help with your money and with your time. Set aside some hours each week or month and dedicate it to help others. If you can put in time at the practice tee, you can spend some time assisting and serving others too. "In all things I have shown you that by working hard in this way we must help the weak and remember the words of the Lord Jesus, how he himself said, 'It is more blessed to give than to receive'" (Acts 20:35).

3. For your kindness. Let your light shine all the time. Speak nice words to people and smile often. I remember a man who was not kind to a woman at the counter when his flight was canceled. The cancellation was not her fault, but the passenger took his frustrations out on her. I don't know his name, but I recall how horrible he treated her. I

also recall the grace she showed in not responding. Don't be like him. Kindness matters when you encounter a waitress or an Uber driver. Demonstrate kindness with words and with gifts. "Above all, keep loving one another earnestly, since love covers a multitude of sins" (1 Peter 4:8).

4. For your praise. Are there people you remember who praised God in church? That's not a bad legacy to leave. But of course, live that lifestyle when you go to work or the golf course. Don't be that guy who hurls the club in the water after an errant shot. "With my mouth I will give great thanks to the Lord; I will praise him in the midst of the throng" (Psalm 109:30).

5. For your testimony. Live what you believe. If you are a Christian, represent the Kingdom the best you can. You will have days when you don't make the cut but come back the next day and sink that twenty-two-footer for birdie. Be one who encourages and a person of inspiration. Get things done, but always give God His glory.

Corey prepared his entire professional life for that one moment. He did not wake up on that final Sunday and think he was going to hit the shot of his life, but the moment presented itself.

You must always be in position to do the same. Be ready. Leave a legacy.

Chapter 28

WHY ARE YOU HERE?

Jack Nicklaus

And be not conformed to this world: but be ye transformed by the renewing of your mind, that ye may prove what is that good, and acceptable, and perfect, will of God.
—Romans 12:2 (KJV)

You may struggle to find your calling or gift, as I did for many years. But for others, they may know what they want to do early in life, and that is fantastic.

Jack Nicklaus knew at an early age that he was blessed with talent and ability to play golf.

Don't get me wrong, he had to work hard to fine-tune his craft, but there is no doubt he was made to play golf.

Over his career, he won 73 PGA tournaments, which included 18 Major championships, the most of any player.

"I'm here because I made a few four-foot putts," he told me with a chuckle in Dublin, Ohio, home of The Memorial Tournament of which he is the host. "None of this would have ever happened if I had not made those putts— and a few twenty-footers too."

Awards don't just happen, they are earned.

I knew moments after I hit a golf ball that the tour was *not* in my future. There were things I wanted to do but knew I did not possess the talent or did not have the gift. I took some lessons, but I still knew that was as good as I would get.

I stumbled into my first sports writing gig out of college and had a blast. It was something I never envisioned. I won some awards right off of the tee box, but financial issues encouraged me to pursue other options.

For years I struggled to find what God wanted for me. It took me until I was fifty years old to find my calling. Writing.

Writing was something I did for a living for a few years, but it was not a ministry.

My wife encouraged me to enter the Christian writing world, and the Lord affirmed it when several doors opened for me.

For Jack, he knew his calling when he was a youngster. For me, it was midlife. God's timing is perfect.

What are your talents? What can you do for the Lord? What is your purpose in life?

> For I know the thoughts that I think toward you, saith the LORD, thoughts of peace, and not of evil, to give you an expected end.
>
> —Jeremiah 29:11 (KJV)

Tee It Up

If you are like me, you may have searched for years to find your calling or purpose in life. Maybe you know what God wants for you and that's fantastic. Or perhaps you have not discovered what the Lord wants you to do for Him. And that's fine too. And it's OK to become frustrated a little if you don't have confirmation yet. You may want to preach but are not called. The biggest mistake you can make is to force the issue and give in to your own thoughts and your own selfish desires. I would encourage you not to do something because *you* want to do it.

Go for the Green

Everyone wants to find their purpose in life and work for the Lord. Or at least they should. If you are content with being on the practice tee or practice green, you need to have a chat with your caddie who wants you to be a contender. You may struggle and not know what you are supposed to do.

Some tips to find your purpose in life and how to use your God-given talents to spread the good news of Christ:

1. Be patient. I hope it doesn't take you fifty years like it did for me, but if that's the case, be patient. There may be a reason why you wait. For me, it wasn't until I shed the stubbornness of self and realized this is what God wants me to do. "But if we hope for that we see not, then do we with patience wait for it" (Romans 8:25 KJV).

2. Pay attention. You have interests that grab your attention, whether it's sports, cooking, or travel. Let your passion direct you toward your calling but don't be stubborn and not accepting of other

areas. If you love cooking, then your interest of being of use might be to volunteer and prepare food for people. If you love to travel, maybe God wants you on the mission field. The point here is to stay in areas that interest you and wait for the Lord to open the door.

3. Seek counsel. Talk to your pastor or Sunday school teacher about your interest or desire to be used by God. Maybe seek out someone you respect and pray about your desire. Be open to advice and never say never. "Where no counsel is, the people fall: but in the multitude of counsellors there is safety" (Proverbs 11:14 KJV).

4. Pray for wisdom. If you played golf in high school or college and went through a funk where you could do nothing right, you sought the advice and instruction from your coach. Or maybe you hired a golf club professional or watched those clips on YouTube for suggestions. The same goes for your calling. In prayer, ask the Lord for direction. When you ask, be prepared to listen. Stay away from giving God suggestions. He will direct your path in His time and not yours. Remember the first suggestion? Be patient. Your heavenly Father wants to be involved in your decision. "But seek ye first the kingdom of God, and his righteous-ness; and all these things shall be added unto you" (Matthew 6:33 KJV).

5. Let go of self-desires. This is not about you. This is about how to glorify God and lead others to Him.

God will not bless you if you try to honor the Lord when He is not in the action. If you want to sing but lack the ability, others will not be blessed, and you will look like a fool. Take your eyes off others and release any self-serving desires over to Christ.

When you find your true calling from God, your journey will begin. It may be in a field you never wanted to pursue. Stay open to God's leading and be willing to do whatever He wants you to do.

When your calling is revealed to you, do it with everything that is in you to be the best you can with your talent.

Chapter 29

TODAY IS THE DAY FOR JOY

Stewart Cink

This is the day that the LORD has made;
let us rejoice and be glad in it.

—Psalm 118:24

When I write a devotional book based on interviews with athletes, like this one, I often wait a lot—for appointments and interviews.

I must wait for the event, such as The Memorial Tournament, or a baseball or football game to attend. When the day finally arrives, I still wait.

I must wait for the opportunity to present itself for me to speak with my intended target.

And I must wait on the athlete or player and respect their time.

When I started to plan for this book, I knew I wanted to talk with Stewart for this project. But I also had to wait for him to arrive at the course and for that moment to appear, if it did at all. Sometimes I will wait for hours and leave without the interview, unless I can schedule an appointment. But that can be laborious too.

During the day, I spoke with volunteers who possessed some knowledge of when certain players come off the course.

One gentleman told me that Stewart usually comes to the practice green late in the afternoon during the week of the tournament after most spectators have gone for the day.

Around 4:30 p.m. I had just finished an interview with Cameron Tringale and had given up on Stewart. I decided to head back to the hotel. The crowd was dwindling and scattered throughout the practice green area.

And there he was. Stewart had just completed his time at the driving range and was headed toward the practice putting green next to the clubhouse.

I asked if he had a few moments to talk about his faith and he invited me to "walk and talk."

He told me without hesitation that his faith was the most important factor in his life.

"It enables me to feel peace and joy in my life even when the golf ball is not agreeing with my club face and not going where I want it to go," he said. "I don't look for peace and joy and happiness from golf because I know I cannot depend on that to truly sustain the kind of peace I'm looking for. Don't take that wrong, I love playing and winning and competing out here, but the peace and joy that I experience as a Christian is available to everybody all the time. You just have to ask for it from the Lord. It's available upon request and you don't have to wait for certain circumstances."

Stewart and I stood in the roped-off section in front of the putting green and talked about the goodness of the Lord. He thanked me for the time and for the questions because he doesn't field the topic of salvation often.

"We install our peace and joy because of our faith in Jesus Christ, it's really that easy," he added.

You will seek me and find me, when you seek me with all your heart.

—Jeremiah 29:13

Tee It Up

No one likes to wait. But you probably do when you are in line at Texas Roadhouse for that perfect steak. Or you glance at your watch when you sit in the doctor's lobby and wait for your name to be called. Or you might try to pass the time if you have bouts of insomnia and wait on the sandman to lull you off to sleep. When you were a child, do you remember waiting on your birthday or Christmas Day to arrive? Those days were torture for a little kid. Do you ever wait with excitement? Everyone does at some point in life. The waiting game is a huge portion of life.

Go for the Green

But what about joy and happiness? Do you wait for those moments? When that steak comes out just the way you ordered, does that make you happy? Are you satisfied? What about if it is overcooked? What then? Do you send it back or devour it anyway? Or how did you feel or react when you tore open that present on your birthday only to find it was something you didn't want or even know what it was? Where was your joy? Things cannot provide sustained happiness and joy. Only God can provide that. Some ways to have joy and happiness all the time:

1. Count your blessings. Everyone experiences trials and heartaches. But if you focus on those, you will not be happy or have joy. If you make out a list of pros and cons, you might find the good outnumbers the bad. You might have something negative happen to you throughout the course of the day, but in the end, you can find more joy and happiness in the fact that God loves you and will always be by your side. "The LORD bless you and keep you; the LORD make his face to shine upon you and be gracious to you; the LORD lift up his countenance upon you and give you peace" (Numbers 6:24–26).

2. Give to others. You might ask, "How can this make me happy?" I would encourage you to spend time helping those who are not as blessed as you and see how that makes you feel. It will encourage you to take inventory of yourself and see that you are blessed beyond measure. "But if anyone has the world's goods and sees his brother in need, yet closes his heart against him, how does God's love abide in him?" (1 John 3:17).

3. Worship. Stewart enjoys the accolades and applause from fans when he hits a good shot or wins a tournament. That's recognition that he did something good. He reached a milestone and reaped the benefits of a trophy and cash prizes. When you worship Christ in song or lifted arms,

you are telling Him "great job" and thanking Him for His blessings.

> All the earth worships you
>> and sings praises to you;
>> they sing praises to your name. (Psalm 66:4)

4. Read. Spend a few moments each morning or evening in the Word of God. This is His love letter or playbook for you to be successful. If you remember receiving or writing letters to your sweetheart, you know how good that made you feel. The Bible is the same. It's His words to you and His expression of love for you. Read it every day. "All Scripture is breathed out by God and profitable for teaching, for reproof, for correction, and for training in righteousness" (2 Timothy 3:16).

5. Adjust your attitude. There might be times of discouragement you go through but don't dwell there long. If something terrible happens to you or someone you love, it's OK to allow your human emotions to come out. But turn your focus on the goodness of the Lord. You may not understand the circumstances but know that the Lord will carry you through the bunkers and rough grass onto the smoothness of the green. "Humble yourselves before the Lord, and he will exalt you" (James 4:10).

I had to wait for my time with Stewart, and it was worth it. Sometimes when you wait, good things happen. Don't force them but allow the Lord to set the stage. He did that for me. But I am glad I don't have to wait for interviews to happen to make me happy.

I can have joy and peace *now* through my experience with Christ . . . and so can you.

Chapter 30

THAT ONE GLORIOUS DAY

Del Duduit

For the grace of God has appeared, bringing salvation for all people, training us to renounce ungodliness and worldly passions, and to live self-controlled, upright, and godly lives in the present age, waiting for our blessed hope, the appearing of the glory of our great God and Savior Jesus Christ, who gave himself for us to redeem us from all lawlessness and to purify for himself a people for his own possession who are zealous for good works.

—Titus 2:11–14

Let me begin by emphatically stating that *I am not in any way* a professional golfer. But I do have an inspirational story.

I am your average bogey golfer on a good day. And a good day for me is when all the planets align and everyone parts the highways to make way for me on the way to the course. That's in a perfect world, which also includes a hot fudge sundae.

But this is a broken world, so I'll conclude this devotional book with my own personal, yet true, golf story.

My family and I were on vacation in Sarasota, Florida, a few years back. I made a tee time to play golf with my youngest son at Rolling Green Golf Course. The day was a scorcher. When we teed off around 10:00 a.m., the temperature was already about 88 degrees and climbing.

I blew through every fairway and played like I wore a blindfold with one hand tied to my side. It was miserable. I was hot. Sweaty. And there wasn't enough room on the scorecard for all those large numbers.

The rough lived up to its word. My clubs turned every time I tried to make solid contact, and I chunked enough grass to fill up a small pickup. I quit keeping score. I can play golf, but this day was awful.

The next day, I awoke and decided to take on that course again. My son thought I needed therapy. But he went with me, probably to keep me from throwing all my clubs in a lake.

When we arrived, I left my driver and 3 wood in the van.

I teed off with either a 3 iron, 4 iron, or 5 iron. I kept the ball in the fairways most of the day. I gave myself shots at the green and hit several greens in regulation—a complete turnaround from the day before.

On the par-3 seventeenth hole, I tossed my approach into a green-side bunker. After I finished the hole with a double bogey, I was determined to do better.

I did. I birdied the eighteenth. When I tallied up the scorecard, I smiled. A true miracle. My first and only 69.

I did not allow the discouragement and failure of the day before to stop me from conquering the course. I knew I could play better if I adjusted and simply played the course.

Granted, I did not count on a couple of long putts to fall for birdies, but when you are on a roll good things happen.

That one glorious day has kept me going back to the golf course—any course—time and time again. I know I'll probably never break 70 again. But at least I can say I did it, and I have a picture of the signed card framed on my office wall as proof.

You can do the same when it comes to life. You can toss your bad days aside and focus on accepting the simple gift of salvation that Christ has to offer.

Leave all your cares and the clubs that will steer you off course in your vehicle. Cast your burdens on Him, and He will bring you out of the bunker of life for a birdie.

You can experience that glorious day when the Lord saves you.

Let not your hearts be troubled. Believe in God; believe also in me. In my Father's house are many rooms. If it were not so, would I have told you that I go to prepare a place for you? And if I go and prepare a place for you, I will come again and will take you to myself, that where I am you may be also.

—John 14:1–3

Tee It Up

Have you ever had one of those days on the course that I described above? I'm talking about the tough one where I struggled. Nothing went right, and the misery was unbearable. But when you look back, you also have enjoyed the thrill of shooting under par. Maybe you have, and that's great. For me, it was my once-in-a-lifetime when all aspects of my game came together. Now let's change course and discuss life. Are there times when you know you need to make a change? I'm talking about the time I left my big clubs in the van. I knew that was the best choice. But what choices do you have when life tosses you into the rough? In golf, the rough will often "grab" the club and it will twist in your hands when you make contact. When that happens, you can't control the ball. It may go three feet, or it may sail in a different direction and even find water. There is a simpler way.

Go for the Green

Christ made salvation so easy that a child can understand. Golfers and those who interview players tend to make the game more difficult than it is. They talk about wind trajectory and moving the ball inside and out and what line to place it on so it will trickle down to the hole. Golf is by far the toughest sport to play well. But it's only a game. It's over in a few hours. Life is also short. What clubhouse do you plan to enter for eternity? Here is the game plan if you are not yet ready to go to heaven when you clean your clubs for the last time.

1. Realize you need a Savior. My pastor once said the hardest part of his job is to get people to realize they are lost and going to hell. No one is perfect. Not even Jack Nicklaus or Tiger Woods. You need

a heavenly Father. "For all have sinned and fall short of the glory of God" (Romans 3:23).

2. Repent of your sins. This is when you acknowledge your sins before the Lord. You don't have to list them one by one in front of nosy people. All you need to do is cry out to the Lord with a humble heart and tell Him that you are a sinner. "Repent therefore, and turn back, that your sins may be blotted out" (Acts 3:19).

3. Ask God for forgiveness. This is the only way to heaven. God will forgive you if you ask with a humble and honest heart. The Lord is not a genie in a bottle or a wishing well. You can't just use Him for that reason. Christ paved the way for you to have eternal life, but you must act on this and seek Him. "For God so loved the world, that he gave his only Son, that whoever believes in him should not perish but have eternal life" (John 3:16).

4. Learn and grow. The only way this happens is to read the Word of God every day, pray to the Lord daily, and attend church on a regular basis. You cannot improve your golf game if you don't go to the range and get on the course. If you want to become better, you put in the time. The same goes for your spiritual growth. Practice.

5. Follow, obey, and enjoy. Seek the Lord's will and obey His commandments and His will for your life. Just like golf, you must have patience. Find a group of like-minded people and stay connected.

Become involved and stay the course. Weather the bad days and enjoy the good ones. Even though you are saved, this doesn't mean your life will be worry free or without problems. It means you have a source of power to handle the double bogeys. The Christian life is the best one to live. Go have fun.

If you need a prompt, try this: Dear Lord Jesus, I know that I am a sinner, and I ask for Your forgiveness. I believe You died for my sins and rose from the dead on the third day. I turn from my sins and invite You to come into my heart and life. I want to trust and follow You as my Lord and Savior. In Your Name. Amen.

If you prayed this prayer, you just birdied every hole on the course.